Real Influencers

Manufactured in the United States of America.

1 2 3 4 5 6   27 26 25 24 23 22

Library of Congress Control Number: 2022946022

Paperback ISBN: 978-1-5873-691-3
Ebook ISBN: 978-1-58731-692-0

∞ The paper used in this publication meets the minimum requirements of the American National Standard for Information Sciences – Permanence of Paper for Printed Materials, ANSI Z39.48-1984.

St. Augustine's Press
www.staugustine.net

Real Influencers

Fourteen Disappearing Acts Th
Left Fingerprints on History

KENNETH WEISBRODE

ST. AUGUSTINE'S PRESS

South Bend, Indiana

For James E. Goodby

Contents

Contents

PREFACE

About twenty years ago I was asked by a friend to help with some research for a British university. I knew nothing about the topic, Iranian nuclear technology, but the pay was good and the job was easy. One day a few months into the project, my friend telephoned with some urgency: There were a few names that needed filling-in. I dropped everything and did as I was asked, thinking little about it. The next morning there was an article on the front page of the *New York Times* about this exact subject, with a couple of the sentences I had written reprinted verbatim and delivered as settled opinion. I had no idea how or why they ended up there. But, I wondered, is that how it's done?

I've thought about this incident off and on ever since—and the "it" above, which is influence. A history teacher of mine once said it's impossible to prove, and therefore a risky subject for anyone to take on. I believed him, but that hasn't stopped me from thinking about it, almost obsessively, making it the subject of my own work over the years. It cannot be proved; but it cannot be denied either. So how do we measure influence? How do we detect it? And how, if we are determined to be more than mere observers of life, do we exercise it?

I have used the convenient and predictable term *fingerprint* in the subtitle of this book. A fingerprint is usually not visible to the naked eye; a chemical solution and training are needed to detect it. It does not last forever, but it does last after the deed is done or the body that had been present is gone. It is, in other words, a temporary piece of history, not as fleeting as events themselves may

1

be, and only in the smallest of ways a record of those events. Yet it exists for a time, and therefore has a history that may be significant.

The notion of the fingerprint is often used in literature and popular culture in such a manner. My own acquaintance with it (and the concept of influence) came by way of an unpublished memoir with the title, *How Little Wisdom: Memoirs of an Irresponsible Memory ... Written Solely But, Hopefully, for the Entertainment and Perhaps Edification of the Family; Diplomatic Memoirs are as Boring as Other People's Snapshots or Operations.* A portion of it was later published with the title "Fingerprints on History." The author was a diplomat, Theodore Achilles, who happened also to be one of the principal authors of the North Atlantic Treaty. Nobody would know that had they not taken the time to find his fingerprints in the form of his initials and name on accompanying memoranda in official archives; or if by some chance they stumbled across his memoir, which I had done thanks to the generosity of an acquaintance who possessed a copy. But I had also known of Mr. Achilles. I had once worked for the organization that he founded, alongside a granddaughter, as it happens, and knew a thing or two about his career, although he had died a few years before all that. So I had a bit of the solution before finding the fingerprint, to be fair.

A good friend of Mr. Achilles was a man I knew well. His name was John Gray. He was one of the most intelligent people I have ever known and had a great influence on me, or so I feel. He was an engineer and one of the youngest to work on the Manhattan Project. From there he ran the first civilian atomic energy station, at Shippingport, Pennsylvania. He also worked for some time for Admiral Hyman Rickover in the U.S. Navy.

John Gray was one of those men who are stereotypically described as soft-spoken, inconspicuous, yet almost Yoda-like figures. He was not tall, walked with a stoop, and usually wore a Greek sailor's cap. One could pass him a hundred times on the street and fail to notice his face. He was not the sort of person who made an entrance. He spoke to me usually in short, sometimes cryptic sentences. Often he'd only nod or wink. The only really distinctive thing about his appearance or physical presence was the blueness of his eyes.

Somehow, I came to sense that John Gray knew just about everybody, in the energy industry, in the nuclear business, in private equity (he used to buy and sell companies), and probably in one or two other areas. I also came to feel that people like him, however unique they could seem to an impressionable young (or not so young) person, they were a dime a dozen in an imperial capital like Washington, D.C. How exactly do they wield influence? Where is the power in such influence; or what is the difference between power and influence, and why does the difference matter? Where do they acquire their ability to influence? Or do they just appear to have it?

John Gray had a simple method for influence: He once told me that about all you could hope for in life was to have real influence at the margins. He never told me what "real influence" and "margins" were, but he planted a seed in my thinking about the subject. My interest in the concept of influence, and the rationale for this little book of portraits, derives from that seed. I am less interested in figures of so-called great influence: the people who move mountains by inspiring millions of followers and altering the fate of the world. We know their names. Or in momentary influence of the contemporary variety, which seems to me less about influence and more about persuasion or compulsion. I am interested instead in a quieter type of influencer. Not necessarily more discreet or even less ambitious, but more deliberate in exercising influence at the margins and thereby leaving a lasting fingerprint, not only on the margins but sometimes at the center of human affairs.

The influencer in this book is a person who made an art of absence in the trade of cultural and sometimes political capital. The ones in this book represent a range of vocations, from politics to diplomacy to novel-writing, but almost all were cultural entrepreneurs. They were not puppet masters, gray eminences, unsung heroes, or Svengalis, although one or two have been portrayed thus. Rather, their influence is spread by virtue of their willful disappearance, of its perpetuation of a new language and cultural standard, and of their many conscious and unconscious imitators. The reason they had such influence was precisely because a part of their method was to be less visible in order to watch their ideas, habits, and styles proliferate without their names being affixed. If proliferation didn't have an obvious imprint and reflect back on the taker well, so much the better, and so much the better does it happen. In a sense this is maximally hubristic. And deeply non-ascetic in disappearing. Yet, to understand such a modus operandi is necessary today when the proliferating social media influencers are squandering cultural capital so quickly by the simultaneous promotion of their products—above all, themselves.

The selection of people for this book is of course idiosyncratic and personal. Most I knew at one or two steps removed. So, much of what I have written is anecdotal in the way that influence is shared and understood. Some of the people are (or once were) quite well-known public figures, so it isn't quite fair to say they are disappearing acts, but none was really a household name and most are known today only to their devotees. There is also a notable sex imbalance in the selection, and for that I have no excuse other than my own tendency to have experienced more public influence from men than from women. It is not at all meant to suggest that the one is more or less influential than the other, although my rather primitive understanding of today's social media environment tells me that female influencers have a big boost on the males.

I should also note the obvious centering of the selection on

Americans and some Europeans, and mostly on the middle to late twentieth century. The reason is again quite personal: One is supposed to write about what one knows, or as I think Gore Vidal once said, what one thinks one would like to know. In either case, this is a book by a historian but written from the perspective of a memoirist of a certain time and place, which is semi-public America at the turn of the twenty-first century. I recall the years leading up to it less as a tribute—and here I must admit that I began this collection as a study provisionally titled "Homage to Mr. Lovett" (as in Robert Lovett) and then shelved it—than as an open inquiry into the impression and expression of influence, from a sentimental but not uncritical position. I describe the influence of these people in a way that I myself have either felt or seen felt. I could have written portraits of any number of other important influencers: for example, Dorothy Wordsworth (the poet's sister and muse), Bourke Cockran (the orator and politician), Pauli Murray (the lawyer, priest, and activist), Harold Ford (one of the inventors of the National Intelligence Estimate), Marjorie Sewell Cautley (the landscape architect), Subhas Chandra Bose (the Indian nationalist), George Benson (the American confidant of Suharto), Régine Zylberberg (the impresario), John Lord O'Brian (the lawyer and public servant), Robbie Basho (the guitarist), Ann Lowe (the dressmaker), Alvey Adee (the bureaucrat), Pierre Sprey (the military engineer), Sister Parish (the interior designer), Ray Kroc (the fast-food seller), Norman Davis (the diplomat), or Yukio Mishima (the writer) ... or hundreds of like-individuals whose impressions cross my mind from areas of life that are less familiar to me, such as business, entertainment, science, law, and haute couture. Whether you have heard of these people or not, their influence to me would have felt more remote, even academic. I defer to other writers, including academic ones, to do that better than I.

"Get the idea out there, and the publicity will take care of itself." That was another bit of advice I got around the time I knew

John Gray. It is tempting to believe that it is true, even in today's highly egocentric public sphere. This set of portraits is an experiment to find out if the erasure of the personal element might be the most effective way of creating mass-influence. Because of the tendency, whether genuine or feigned, of several of its subjects to wallow in self-deprecation, their influence is meant to be taken at face value. This is not, in other words, a subtle experiment in satire. Someday no doubt there will be one or more books of eminent influencers narrated in the Lytton Strachey mold; but this is not that.

Benjamin Franklin, who knew a thing or two about satire as well as strategic self-deprecation, equated it not with vanity per se, or with hubris, but rather with the pragmatic need to obtain the assent of other people in order to accomplish things in the world. So much the better if they felt the idea was their own, or if they thought you were merely imparting it rather than staking a claim over it. As we'll see with the portrait of Jean Monnet, nearly everyone who uses the tired phrase, "if you want to get something done, let someone else get the credit," almost never gives credit to whomever invented that phrase, be it Monnet or someone else, as if to say, the clever phrase is my own. Such are the ways of having influence at the margins.

In thinking over this book one final idiosyncratic element has occurred to me. It is rather transparently the product of an American member of Generation X and our allegedly semi-detached, semi-wistful, and semi-sardonic outlook on our country in the world in the early part of the twenty-first century. Unlike our own successors, we remember the twentieth century, its ideologies, and its liberation from their straightjacket. Unlike our predecessors, especially the dying but still, remarkably, omnipresent baby boomers, the ideological chip on our shoulder is less heavy, less overdetermined. Part of us wishes we had been born earlier in the American Century to have celebrated all it was said to be; and part of us is very glad to have been spared all that, or at least some of it. But this book is not an epitaph for the twentieth century, nor is it a book about unsung heroes and heroines, or late greats. It is more neutral in that respect, yet still sympathetic toward its subjects and their ways.

This chronological placement is important now that the most frequent mention of influence besides the social media influencers happens in the realm of geopolitics. The era of great ideological conversion is the past. Some people still speak of the American Dream, but now many others speak of the Chinese Dream (and there are, by most approximations, many more Chinese influencers on social media). There may no longer be the same sort of races in armaments, space voyages, or kitchen appliances as there were during the Cold War, but try to tell anyone who works in the creative industries or in retail that there is not an influence race taking place every single day, at all hours. Just as there was once said to be a race for winning the hearts and minds of the non-aligned peoples of the world, so too is there now a race for winning a geopolitical contest understood, fairly or not, with the logic and language of influence.

This larger sense of influence is the underlying theme of this book. Influence has a long complicated history from its effects on individuals as well as nations. At its core, though, it remains what it has always been: a blend of persuasion, inspiration, and pressure that joins the influencer with the influenced in a mutual relationship over time and space. To detect and understand that relationship varies in difficulty; sometimes influence, particularly in appearances, seems obvious. At other times it is barely detectable. Today, the advertisement of geopolitical influence, sometimes called "soft power," as a substitute for "hard" military power has become quite fashionable, at least in most parts of the West as Western electorates have finally come to terms with the fact that their countries have won no major war, with the partial exception of George Bush the Elder's Gulf War (which historians have already begun to call a Pyrrhic victory), since World War II. Yet, "soft power" is nothing new. It usually follows the flag. Which is to say, influence and power are indivisible when the subject is the nation or the empire.

Little of that would have been news to the generation of Americans and their friends around the world who presided over what is now unfashionably called the American Century. It was once and somewhat less unfashionably called the Century of the Common Man. There were millions of such men and women, presiding, influencing, in their own important ways. Their wisdom was of a different hue than the creative appeal of most of today's influencers. What made the "wise men" of that era once so appealing was not simply their cohesion, single-mindedness, and dedication during a moment of great international danger in the late 1940s and 1950s. It was also their endurance in public service, and that they stepped in to help rescue a couple of presidents and the republic from further loss in Vietnam. The latter story, still guided by ideology, has yet to be fully or fairly told, partly because so many of the chroniclers of this period wrote, and are still writing, contemporaneously and therefore subjectively as witnesses and participants. Back then and in subsequent decades, strategic wisdom was measured ever more narrowly with the language of power. But that measurement fails to account for the extent to which the Cold War, which enveloped the Vietnam and other, similar 'wars of liberation,' was, once again, a grand struggle for influence—a struggle which saw influence not by degree so much as by fashionable and popular refinement—over sentimental attachments divided less between the East and the West, and more between the proud and the humiliated, the rich and the poor, the haves and the have-nots, and what one twentieth century historian memorably termed "the forces of order and the forces of movement."

Those divisions became mutual dependencies. Influence traveled in both directions. Someday, it may be said that the Cold War generation of wise men and women, like their Progressive Era predecessors, succeeded in one area most of all: wielding influence over their own generation and those that followed by convincing them to be loyal imitators of language and the terms by which political and related forms of influence were imparted and understood. These were men and women of greater impact later and they may well serve as molders of the modern postwar West, or perhaps of another world which is now emerging.

Mr. Achilles, as it happens, was keen on what he liked to call "the successor generation." He wanted it to carry on his life's work, and he concocted mentorship programs to do that. It was as if he sought a different sort of fingerprint solution: not one to reveal the surviving print but another to make it last longer undetected. Psychologists may debate whether one form of ventured immortality is more egotistical than another, and they should be encouraged. For without the human ego, not much would be accomplished at all. But influence, as the portraits in the pages that follow illustrate, amounts to more than the expression of ego. It has a generous, votive aspect. In some instances it comes simply from a desire to share. It is in that spirit, rather than anything more vainglorious or profound, that I offer this small book.

1. L'inspirateur

JEAN MONNET

Charles de Gaulle called him "l'inspirateur." It was not meant as a compliment. Much has been written about the man called the father of Europe. Monnet spent most of his life shunning credit; and yet today, as already noted, he is credited with the phrase, "If you want to get something done, let someone else take the credit." He put the phrase in someone's mouth, who put it in another's, who put it in General George Marshall's, who may or may not have said it. This was in miniature the modus operandi of Jean Monnet.

Monnet came from Cognac and began his adult life as a cognac merchant for his family firm. This took him to many parts of the world, and North America particularly inspired him at this age. He fell for it for all the usual reasons: the openness, frankness, clarity of purpose. He traveled as far as the Yukon and met many people, but he was clear about the people he most needed to meet. Monnet had a sixth sense for influence; he was able to know whose repeated words mattered most; and he had an impressive capacity to reach such people and endear them to himself.

He was an otherwise mediocre businessman; he kept his family's firm afloat and also did passably well as a banker. But earning money, which he did well, or losing it, which he also did well, was never really the point. Monnet's great talent was for selling ideas. Whether or not they inspire is something that rests in the eye of the beholder. The point is that people bought them.

For this reason Jean Monnet has also been called an original policy entrepreneur. Like any product, selling a policy requires the right packaging, good timing, a ready market. Monnet's product, European integration, had all these things when it was finally launched after the Second World War. None of it was particularly original. Monnet's contribution was to devise a method for selling his policy that compounded the influence he and it had over time. In other words, he sold a policy that went on to sell itself.

He did that in three ways: first by mastering the packaging and timing, which is to say, the language by which it is known; second by knowing exactly who could be the most useful in certain places; and third by simple repetition. The final element set another template. Today it is an axiom in Washington, D.C. and probably in most other capitals that the simple formula for success in policy entrepreneurship is to repeat just one idea (and no more than one) over and over again but each time with just a bit more glibness. Soon other people do it and the idea becomes a slogan: "arsenal of democracy," "ever closer union," "trust but verify," "end endless wars," "soft power," etc.

This method, which has been described in Monnet's case as a perpetual Kaffeeklatsch, was obviously more than a game of telephone. Monnet himself wrote very little. He spoke. His voice was small and did not carry far on its own; his few attempts at speechmaking were miserable. Others did that for him and in the words he provided to them, often at two, three, or many more mouths removed as if to make him a linguistic Johnny Appleseed.

Monnet never held elected office. His official positions were all appointed. And although some of his titles were important— deputy secretary-general of the League of Nations, head of French planning, and the first president of the High Authority of the European Coal and Steel Community, for example—his greatest influence probably came after 1954 when he held no official title at all. He stepped down from the High Authority and established a non-governmental association or what today we would call a lobby or pressure group called the Action Committee for the United States of Europe. It was multinational, multi-sectoral (with industrialists and union leaders), and multi-party. It produced consensus reports with terms that fit easily into the mouths of politicians, helping them to adhere to policies that served no particular interest (and therefore were difficult to advance individually), but that served the collective interest as Monnet saw it.

Historians like Jean Monnet for reports such as these. They leave behind so many arguments, turns of phrase, and other bits of verbiage that may be found in memoranda, speeches, letters, and conversations lodged in archives. The words can be traced back to Monnet and his remarkable capacity to get others to repeat them. In this instance there were basically two ideas: that nation-states had to integrate their economies and societies in order for both to survive; and that such integration was a progressive force that required constant motion in order to thrive. The reports themselves and nearly everything else (for who can remember the text of foreign minister Robert Schuman's speech on May 9, 1950, announcing the plan to pool the French and German coal and steel industries?) were never as important as Monnet's collaborative capacity had been. His gift and his influence were procedural. They did not produce results so much as they made a way to achieve results, a mentality for achieving them, and a human map for making them stick. When that happened, the results, Monnet claimed, spoke for themselves.

This is what political scientists at the time called "functionalism." No doubt it was, as critics have often claimed, an elite project. Monnet had, after all, started out selling mainly cognac. He took some pride in saying he came from good peasant stock and had the shrewdness to prove it, and this was partly true if one went back a few generations; but his gifts of inspiration and persuasion were confined to a narrow, mainly American or pro-American, elite. He convinced these Americans that he was a different sort of European, one they could do business with, one who understood and flattered their sense of optimism, and one who needed their leverage to persuade other, more cynical, Europeans to do what was in their mutual interest before it was too late. Otherwise, there was never much of a chance that the people throughout Western Europe would cotton to what Monnet was selling. They were only a few generations into knowing the concept of nationalism, and into the sacrifices of blood and treasure it demanded; yet now they were being told that nationalism was a dangerous thing of the past or even a sin. For the people's masters—industrialists, union bosses, politicians, financiers who did not mind thinking about political trends—maybe Monnet had a point, but it was not one most of them cottoned to, either. What he wanted them to do sounded very expensive.

Monnet and his method made use of a few more principles. One was that, as he put it, to spare no indignity to sell a policy. Many times he was dismissed, and sometimes insulted. He carried on. Another was to keep carrying on in spite of setbacks. In 1954 the European Defense Community, a premature passion of Monnet's, was voted down by the French national assembly. It looked as though European integration had been nipped in the bud. Monnet had a stroke and resigned from the High Authority. But he took some more of the long Swiss walks he so liked for thinking, established the Action Committee, and carried on. The following year at Messina several West European ministers gathered and moved ahead with plans to establish the Common Market.

Today it is stylish to call these narratives resilient. Maybe they were. But it may be better to understand them as simply persistent. The salesman who believes in his product and keeps selling, no matter how many doors are slammed in his face. This is what he does. When the customers finally try it and see how well it works, they'll forget their skepticism.

Persistence was at the root of the Monnet method. So was a particular kind of pragmatism. For as much as Monnet was dismissed as a dreamer, and as much as he was admired for his gifts at networking, he was also known to be ruthlessly efficient with people. When they no longer served a useful purpose, he cut them off. Even though a few names unknown to most of us—Jacques van Helmont, Max Kohnstamm, David Bruce, Tommy Tomlinson, Pierre Uri, John McCloy, François Duchêne, Richard Mayne, George Ball—were, within their small transatlantic club, members of a Monnet mafia, they all had particular uses for Monnet. Too much, for some: Duchêne, for example, checked himself into a sanatorium, it was said, to escape Monnet's demands and to recover from the damage they had done to his mental state. Duchêne went on to write a very generous biography of his patron.

Monnet's pragmatism extended to his politics. It would be easy to describe him as a technocrat *avant la lettre*. He was open to working with any party that advanced the policies he sought. This included communists, although in their case he had an additional reason to be cooperative, perhaps, for the Soviet Union was the only country that was willing to make it possible for him to marry his beloved Silvia, who had already been married once before. It was fitting that their marriage took place there in 1934. Here, too, was an instance of pragmatism in the service of passion.

Another Monnet acolyte, the American Henry Owen, had something to add about Monnet's pragmatism. Monnet used to insist, according to Owen, on a rule: Beware of pragmatists. It was not a self-criticism so much as a disaggregation of what pragmatism meant for Monnet. It was a means, and one that he mastered, but the ends must mean something greater than a momentary alignment. Monnet's stated ends were extremely idealistic. He wanted to design and reify a political and economic system that would end war in Europe, specifically, Western Europe, forever. He wanted to find a way to re-engineer political culture so that the nation-state no longer prevailed, or at least no longer prevailed at the expense of other, neighboring nation-states. For him these actions (a word he long favored) were in service of a modern trend or phenomenon, mentioned by various thinkers but ascribed by Monnet to Teilhard de Chardin, which held that human polities, and therefore humanity and human consciousness, advanced in a progressive enlargement alongside the technological capacity to move people, objects, and ideas across ever greater distances with greater efficiency. Monnet was impatient with proponents of world government—they offended his pragmatism—but he shared this basic belief in sociopolitical growth with many of them. And he saw political pragmatists (Gaullists and other nationalists) as tough obstacles, if only because they were much better salesmen with the common voter than he.

Nevertheless, today the name of Jean Monnet is familiar, almost entirely in Europe, and less as the name of an historical figure than as the namesake of bursaries, fellowships, academic centers, schools, and policy institutes. The people who established and benefit from them invoke Monnet's name as a synonym for Europeanism, which perhaps is what Monnet would want. Except that Monnet's obsession with abjuring credit, his anti-ego (which in reality was a form of superiority complex regarding the ego) raises a doubt here. For Monnet also tended to abjure not only nationalism but also patriotism. He was in his own way a firm patriot of France, and then of Europe, but he long resisted talk of that sort. He spoke of material interests, benefits, possibilities, plans; and left the spiritual attachments and paeans to others. Today he would probably take pride in all that the European Union has become, but would insist as only he could (which is to say, ad nauseam), that the point of it all was to make peace and to advance the cause of humanity more than it was to celebrate and promote Europe or really European prosperity for its own sake.

It is important therefore to remember that "Mr. Europe" during his own lifetime was celebrated more among the policy elite of the United States than in most parts of Europe, where he was regarded with suspicion, even (or especially) in the United Kingdom, of which and of whose government and people he was very fond. Today he is barely known at all the United States, but in truth he was as much an Atlanticist as a Europeanist. Or perhaps one should say, transatlanticist for the number of times Monnet crossed the ocean and for the number of friendships and associations—with bankers, merchants, government officials, lawyers, and journalists—he tended over so many decades. The naming of his action committee for the "United States of Europe" was no accident, and, at the insistence of his friend and lawyer George Ball, the Battle Hymn of the Republic was played at his funeral in 1979.

The point in recalling Monnet's open geopolitics is to underscore his influence, which is again what the social scientists call functional, path-dependent, and supra-territorial. Or as he liked to say, moving from sitting across the table from one another to sitting on the same side and facing the common problem together. On paper or in the mouth of an acolyte several times removed, such a mantra can sound silly, but Monnet had a quasi-mystical way of making it sound profound as well as true. His approach to problems—talking them through in small groups that went on to proliferate, always emphasizing the possible over the probable, and to do so collectively, collaboratively, in the manner of an atelier— became the predominant transatlantic policy method of the latter twentieth century in so many government offices, think tanks, and academic seminars with their own action committees, working groups, and the like. So much so that it reached the state of an axiom as a way to "draw strength by imposing its internal consensus on others." It's not possible to prove that Monnet invented this method; it predated him, of course; but he energized and catalyzed it to such an extent that it became less of an art or a craft than a human science that might be replicated, on principle, anywhere.

That his method had the added advantage of knitting together policy elites on both sides of the Atlantic for at least three generations is significant in itself, although Monnet probably would not be surprised to see how quickly the tapestry would unravel. It happened already several times during his own lifetime. But each time he paused, took a walk in the Swiss mountains, and thought. Then he began to talk.

2. The Diplomat
EVANGELINE BRUCE

The courtier is a figure formed out of the ambivalence of power. Her own power is derivative of her access to the court and her insider knowledge thereof. Yet her influence over the court is, in theory, unlimited. The more power one has, the lonelier one is, or so the powerful often say, which is why every court has courtiers.

In the age of the Enlightenment the female courtier, still sometimes called a courtesan, acquired or rather advanced a more licit character and two additional aspects: a public intellect and a public/private network. Her influence on power thus came not only from her access to it and her capacity to exert influence behind palace gates, but also and just as importantly in the world immediately outside, among the literati and real or would-be cognoscenti. Her own social world, which she tended like a champion gardener, was called a salon and she, the salonnière. Its members were carefully chosen and cultivated; the rules were hers alone; the settings were her drawing rooms, her dining rooms, and her bedrooms; her currency and her passion was influence, not only over the powerful but also over their minds, mores, language, voice, and imagery. These women and their salons became nothing short of institutions.

The modern female courtier, her independent mind and influence notwithstanding, usually derived her place through attachment, if mainly nominal, to a powerful man. Madame de Staël was the daughter of the richest banker in Europe. The Princess Lieven was the wife of a prominent Russian diplomat; Pamela Berry was the daughter of a great Tory politician and married to the owner of the *Daily Telegraph*. Each of these women and so many others like them used the men in their lives to attain a position that wielded influence and power over men, but never, somehow, threatened them as men, or the role of men, in their mutual worlds.

Evangeline Bell Bruce was an Anglo-American courtier of the middle twentieth century. She was the daughter of an American diplomat and a British patrician, and the wife of one of the most beloved sons of the Chesapeake gentry and a formidable courtier in his own right, David Bruce, who married her after divorcing the richest woman in America, Ailsa Mellon. (Ailsa had lost her mind, and her family, in presumed sympathy with her long-suffering husband, multiplied his fortune many times over in the divorce.)

Vangie and David were a fashionable team in America at mid-century. He became the only man to be named ambassador in succession to the three top diplomatic posts at the time: Paris, Bonn, and London. She accompanied him to each one. Meanwhile in Washington, she reigned as queen of Georgetown society, which is saying a great deal because like many things in America, particularly Cold War America, Georgetown was supremely, persistently competitive. The women who ran its salons caviled and once or twice even terrified presidents, cabinets, and Congress.

There is little doubt that Vangie would have insisted that to be a silly exaggeration. She was only the wife of a man whom 99 percent of Americans had never heard of. Yes, she threw nice dinner parties; she liked to read and write, and had nice friends, so the conversation at the table was pleasing; her houses, her three children, and her dogs were all as modest and as middlebrow as nearly everything else in democratic America—to be admired, maybe praised, but not championed or ever worshipped.

Americans conform, or so it is said, which includes conforming to the stereotype of everything not being what it seems. For Vangie, that was the case, again, many times over. Although her partnership with David was successful, her family life was a misery. Her children detested her, complained about her neglect, and went on to lead sad, and in at least one case, tragic, lives of their own. Her only daughter, Sasha, was murdered in cold blood at her parents' Virginia farm. It was said that the murder, and the bungled effort to solve it, ruined David. His glorious career was nearly over anyway, but it ended more abruptly than it probably would have otherwise. Vangie betrayed less of the damage. Georgetown society, or at least her version of it, had already declined by then, the mid-1970s. The coming to power of the Reagans restored a bit of its standing in the following decade but it became sequined, emphasizing style and attraction, yes, but not as it was at the height of the Cold War when Georgetown represented and wielded real power and influence. There is a certain paradox in this chronology: The reign of one part of élite society was very short—by most accounts only about fifteen years long, from the mid-1940s to the early 1960s—yet the lineages and the linkages persist much longer, so as to give the impression that social history, of the United States in particular, is remarkably compact. An easy example may be found in Donald Trump, whose rise to prominence in American public life was much aided by his lawyer, Roy Cohn, who had also been the prosecutor of the Rosenbergs and the lawyer of Senator Joseph McCarthy. Television makes the linkages seem even starker. There is a now notorious episode of the discussion program, Crossfire, on CNN which featured Mr. Trump in a conversation with the two hosts about the writer Tom Wolfe. One host was Tom Braden, an early scion of the Central Intelligence Agency with a wife who fit comfortably in the Georgetown pantheon; the other was Pat Buchanan, Richard Nixon's hothead speechwriter. There, in a nutshell as Americans like to say, was the rise, decline, and fall of the American Century.

Georgetown was close to its center, geographically as well as chronologically and spiritually. The small neighborhood promotes its own peculiar timelessness: The brick houses are old by American standards (dating mainly to the middle 1800s); the streets are tidy and narrow; only a few "mansions" dot the district, and nearly all look out of place amid the row houses. Georgetown had originally been a district of slave quarters, semi-detached from the main part of Washington, D.C. (as it still is, for no subway lines reach there). The houses lie gradually on a slope to the canal that runs alongside the Potomac River; the canal and its towpath are pretty, but also somewhat menacing in their place and feeling of depth at the bottom of the slope; and to Washingtonians of Vangie's generation, they recall the murder there of Mary Pinchot Meyer, the wife of another CIA scion and colleague of Tom Braden, as well as the favorite mistress of John F. Kennedy ... another murder which, in its own way, remains unsolved.

The salonnières of Georgetown went by the strange name of "hostess." Even Katharine Meyer Graham (no relation to Mary), who eventually took over Vangie's mantle and reigned over what was left of Georgetown (from her much larger house) into the 1990s, was called a hostess, despite being the owner and proprietor of the *Washington Post*. With Graham and her central role in the demise of Richard Nixon from the Watergate scandal, Georgetown's power went from semi- to super-public. But it had already been in decline, a trend which Georgetown society usually dated back to the assassination of its favorite president, John F. Kennedy, and the suicide of Kay Graham's husband, Phil, each one taking place in 1963. It was in decline because, while its social power appeared intact or even greater, its influence had begun to wane. Simply put, Georgetown was tarnished with tragedy. It had become less fashionable.

What did it mean to be a hostess? Vangie always said she hated the word. "Socialite" came a close second. To her they meant nothing other than a lady who throws parties. That she did, but they were means to something greater—her and her husband's joint diplomatic career, and the national interest which it served—and not charming ends in themselves. That she may have pressed this point sincerely does not make it true, but it helps to understand how she wielded whatever influence she did. Every guest list, seating arrangement, menu, and so on were selected with that alchemic aim in mind. Vangie must have imagined herself as a human biochemist, mixing and matching associations in combination to produce optimal, diplomatic results. The impulse of such positioning may well have been quasi-scientific, but the method and the mind of it were pure art. Here it may also be important to note that before Vangie became the great chatelaine of Georgetown and Paris, etc., she had been a translator working for spies.

David and Vangie met in London during the war. Both worked for the Office of Strategic Services, predecessor to the CIA. And before becoming ambassador and ambassadress to a series of countries, Vangie and David lived high in Paris when the latter was the representative there of the Marshall Plan, which came close to being a civilian viceroy. Both were Francophiles anyway: David by way of his experience in both world wars (and of his palette); Vangie by way, mainly, of her ear and her mind, and of her taste in books. She wrote one of her own which she spent many years researching: a portrait of the union of Napoleon and Josephine, called *An Improbable Marriage*. David's power over the French government did not quite reach that level, but he was considered virtually a member of the cabinet, whereas Vangie's Parisian salon was every bit as vibrant as the one in Georgetown. It was the same salon, really, only transposed along with her across the Atlantic, as it would be, with a short-lived exception in Beijing, throughout her semi-official life.

There is a small portrait of her in this vein in Nancy Mitford's book, *Don't Tell Alfred*. The American diplomat's wife in that story wields nearly unmatched power; one need only invoke her name in implying that her husband wants this or that policy or decision, and it was as good as done, for nobody dared disappoint her. It is a nice portrait, but it perhaps intentionally overstates the point of Vangie's influence. The influence of the courtier comes from the power of fashion. Policies and actions may be fashionable, surely, but they are the effects, not the root causes, of potent fashionability. Their power comes from being associated with it, not from being part of it. To restate this point in a more specific way, the wife of a diplomat from one of the world's most powerful countries, the United States, did not represent that country or its power so much as its appeal at that particular place and time. To be pro-American was not to be enamored with, or in favor of, its power or even its culture, but rather its fashion as represented in the figure of individual, attractive Americans who caught everyone's attention.

The United States is not the only representative polity in the world, but it was perhaps in the latter half of the twentieth century the one that took virtual representation to a fashionable extreme. The wielding of such representation took place overseas as much as it did back in Georgetown. Both members of this marriage, but especially Vangie, appeared to others as they imagined such a person ought to appear; and they imagined this because they had a representative example to draw from. Well bred, well educated, well spoken, well dressed, well mannered, well watered, and well fed, Vangie and her husband impressed as self-appointed noble emblems of a republican empire, which, as the saying goes, dared not speak its name. They were just citizens like any other, after all. Just a bit more polished than the Joneses.

Yet within their small world, they carried as much influence as any Renaissance courtier, if only because their ilk was rare, and defied stereotypes of the quiet or ugly American. Their form and style were in that sense as aspirational as the language of their country's founding documents, which is to say it not only reflected what certain postwar elites aspired to be, but also represented continuous works in progress in their own right and in the name of a diplomatic tradition that was among the youngest in the Western world. But like many other aspects of their country's culture, Vangie's influence was fleeting. She is little known today, even in Georgetown, except as the original benefactor of a halfway house on the other side of the city devoted to abandoned and neglected teenagers. It carries the name of her deceased daughter, Sasha.

3. The Cosmopolite
ARMINIUS VÁMBÉRY

Vámbéry! How might one compose an ode to this remarkable man? To describe him is difficult enough. He was the matryoshka man; the man of multiple origins and guises; the human embodiment of geographical mélange; or a human palimpsest, at once eternal and variable by gradations and distinctions. Or maybe just as another fortunate scholar who managed to place himself in the right places and the right times, that is, as another lord of the fortunate conjunction.

But what fortune. And what a conjunction. Vámbéry, born Hermann Bamberger (or Wamberger) in Hungary in 1831 (or 1832), arrived at the point when the promoters of imperialism had reached the zenith for that particular ideology as regards the non-European world (first Asia, then Africa). They demanded it and got it. The Habsburg Empire in which he was born, with its Dual Monarchy of Austria-Hungary, did not partake in that particular zenith, content, it would seem, to dwell on lands closer to home. It would finally be brought to its knees by other empires. He arrived, then, in a world in which great imperial rivalries contended for mastery among themselves and with rival passions: national, religious, and others no less fervent.

Vámbéry's great achievement was to weave for himself a public role and posture that took maximum advantage from those rivalries while purporting at the same time to supersede them in the name of peace, humanity, knowledge, wisdom, and all the other (no less fervent) qualities that—at the same time, alas—dominated not only the Age of European High Imperialism but also nearly the entire Victorian era. That era underwrote all those qualities in the two or three decades that preceded the Great War and marked their own culmination of a kind: of the *Pax Europaea* that was neither peaceful nor so much about Europe as it was about extending European rule (including European rivalries) about as far as they could go. This was Napoleon's world *sans* Napoleon, in which rivalrous imperial nations claimed what they could, each and every one with its manifest destiny whose own origins lay in the particular character of the nation, that is, the people.

Vámbéry offers to posterity the obverse of that contradiction. A textbook cosmopolite, he went about uncovering, planting, and celebrating roots wherever he could. His great influence was upon the European imagination at the turn of a new, more violent century, an imagination that regarded progress to be inseparable from civilization as spread through the mastery of human knowledge alongside a glorification of the rich interpenetration of human cultures. Vámbéry showed how, in mastering language, one could master the imperial narrative, as one would say today. By his various enthusiasms he made the non- or quasi-European marches and uplands both a supreme object and subject of curiosity and conviction. In so doing he completed the global romance of European civilization advanced by Napoleon and his various imitators. Vámbéry's adventure may have been the pen that launched a thousand treks, although he almost certainly would have resisted the claim.

He came from Dunaszerdahely, not far from the Danube and today's Hungarian-Slovak border. Vámbéry was lame, Jewish, and poor. His father, an aspiring rabbi, died soon after he was born. By some good fortune, however, he escaped his fate as an apprentice dressmaker to serve as a private tutor, and began acquiring languages. One of the first he learned was Ottoman Turkish, a very difficult language. His Ottoman Turkish became so proficient that he sought work as an interpreter, and traveled to Istanbul, changing his name to Reshid Effendi. This began his career as a great Orientalist and Turcologist. Not only did he speak the language and adopt the nomenclature; he dressed, sang, and socialized as a proper Ottoman subject … and, just as he had done in Hungary, sought and found the right patron. Vámbéry was so successful in the latter quest that eventually he would go on to become a personal adviser to the sultan himself, Abdülhamid II, whom he would visit annually.

Vámbéry would return to Turkey many times, but he was not content to stay there. He went on to Persia, and northward to Turkestan—Bokhara, Herat, Khiva, Meshed, Samarkand—identifying himself anew as a Turkish mystic in search of knowledge, wisdom, and spiritual fulfillment. He was not lying, not entirely. Vámbéry claimed to be in search of the origins of the Hungarian nation, which he identified (he was not alone in this, of course) among the Central Asian hordes. He spoke, sang, listened, and collected—manuscripts, inscriptions, and numerous observations of customs, habits, clothing, dwellings, social institutions, games, prayer rituals, farming techniques, and nearly every other aspect of Central Asian life. He would publish these discoveries as well as some of the first dictionaries for Westerners of the Turkic languages and a number of translations of poetic works from Uzbek, Tatar, Uyghur, Turkmen, etc.

He survived these expeditions; others, accused of spying for one team or another in the vaunted Great Game between Britain and Russia over the allegiance of the khans, emirs, and other potentates in this region of the world, did not. Vámbéry's survival skills were as good as his investigations were profuse and his travelogues, soon to appear in several translations, vivid. So too perhaps was his desire for notoriety. Hungary could not or would not satiate it. Leaving behind his loyal companion and guide in Central Asia, an Uzbek Tatar called Mollah Ishak, he presently made his way to London, took up writing for the newspapers, and became a celebrity. To this he added an academic appointment as a professor of Arabic, Persian, and Turkish at the (Catholic) University of Pest (a rarity at the time for one educated by Protestants). He thus became one of the first academic celebrities, or celebrity academics, the differences between the two categories then, as now, being difficult to parse. To each of them, Vámbéry added that of political activist.

From here Vámbéry graduated from a probable pawn in the Great Game to a knight, or maybe a rook. He chose his side early. The choice did not seem wise initially, for Russia went on to conquer much of Central Asia, and Vámbéry identified Russia as the perennial enemy, not only of the Turkic peoples wherever they reside, but also of Europe, and therefore of civilization. Vámbéry's Russophobia and his celebrity coincided nicely with the turn in British policy away from the dogma of the "Bulgarian horrors" and toward a different alignment, or, rather, back to an older alignment, only now more pronounced, as the guarantor of Ottoman imperial integrity. The policy was not as Turcophilic (or as Russophobic) as Vámbéry may have liked, but it suited for a time. Vámbéry remained a popular writer and lecturer, warning often of the threat of Russia to India, which was mere preface to the danger posed by Russia to much of Asia itself. The future of this vast continent, and probably the entire world, depended upon educating the British public. It appeared that the British public, or a keen portion of it, agreed. Carrying on his habit of gravitating toward the top, Vámbéry soon found himself invited to stay with the Queen at Windsor. Presumably he continued his lecturing there.

All stars begin to fade eventually, and so did Vámbéry's. He even fell out with the sultan, who disliked the portrait Vámbéry had drawn of him in some writings, and may have found their relationship inconvenient once Ottoman policy had begun to draw closer to Russia in the Eastern Mediterranean. Vámbéry describes the cooling of their relationship in his memoir, called *The Story of My Struggles*. The toughest of those may have been to keep his fame intact. Vámbéry is not much remembered today.

Yet he had a great influence. Vámbéry has been credited with some events, from the outcome of the 1878 Congress of Berlin to the initial progress of Theodor Herzl's Zionist campaign. The whispering in the ears of statesmen is impossible to measure, of course: Whether or not the power of his words over the decisions and acts of Lord Salisbury or Abdülhamid is more than a matter of speculation can never be known for certain. That is as it usually is with influence. His influence over public opinion, even in publicity-obsessed late-Victorian Britain, is also impossible to measure, although it is perhaps easier to suggest. The invitations, commissions, appointments, and other advantages extended to Vámbéry do speak for themselves to a certain extent. His main contribution, however, was made—as it was for several others in this compendium—once more in the realm of fashion. Vámbéry's celebrity advanced a certain type of Orientalism. Today one would call it "hands on"; and yet, by his account (though not of course by those of his detractors) it was no less scholarly. Vámbéry depicted himself above all as a scholar in the service of truth. His mission was to uncover and spread truth by making it understandable, clear, simple, and compelling. Some people call this popularization. That was the point.

Orientalism is still today something of a dirty word. Edward Said's book of that title, published nearly half a century ago, saw to that. The word is not popular, at least not nominally. It remains quite popular in deed, above all in Britain and in other Anglophone countries. From the works of Vámbéry's fellow countryman, Aurel Stein, to the interwar vogue of writers such as Peter Fleming, Fitzroy Maclean, Rosita Forbes, and Robert Byron to that of Wilfred Thesiger, Freya Stark, and Eric Newby into the postwar, and to Peter Hopkirk, Peter Frankopan, Christopher de Bellaigue, and

Robert Kaplan today, publishers cannot seem to get enough of Tartary. Nearly all these writers profess a claim to scholarship: in either background or ambition, or sometimes a bit of both, conflating exploration with intellectual tourism. Some are more humble; others are more earnest; but nearly all play at being in search of something or another in the wilds of the Eurasian landmass, just as Vámbéry once was.

It is not sufficient to say this is travel-writing with a twist. Herodotus, Marco Polo, Ruy González de Clavijo, Evliya Çelebi, and many other travelers whose writings are still available may have traversed some of this territory, but if they were in search of anything, it was a good story. Without a good story, Vámbéry would have gotten nowhere, but the story was not sufficient. He imagined himself as a slayer, not a compiler, of popular myths. He sought and found something greater.

What that was is difficult to say. For lack of a better description, it was an alternative, modern worldview. Vámbéry's progenitors were not Marco Polo or Herodotus but later, modern pathfinders, chiefly Alexander von Humboldt, who was probably the most influential of all. Humboldt is known as a Romantic figure but he was also a child of the Enlightenment. His travels and vast body of research were meant not merely to satisfy a curiosity, albeit a curiosity that was profound, but to do something more, to master new knowledge in the way that reason would dictate. In order to master, one must go, see, collect, catalogue, and understand. One had to be, literally, a fellow traveler with that world: to know and therefore to master, and not merely to observe, its people, languages, customs, and so on. Humboldt went west, mainly, and from the Americas constructed the basis of a new, modern, integrated *Cosmos*, which he called it, and which today's vogue calls a global consciousness. Vámbéry went in the other direction and, to a lesser but no less important extent, did the same.

Interconnectedness does sound very much like a twentieth or even twenty-first century concept. So do most words that begin similarly: integration, interrelationship, interdependence, interpenetration, etc. Internationalism and all that went with it, including, of course, cross-cultural exchange, was the great conceptual gift of the middle twentieth century. Vámbéry may well have been ahead of his time, but not by much.

With today's politically correct approach to globalization, which is at once the promoter and the destroyer of the past century's civilized internationalism, the *modus operandi* of a nineteenth-century figure such as Vámbéry presents a quandary. What does one make of his changing identities? Is it really an offense in Orientalist terms to play by his rules, that is, by what is again today called cultural appropriation, and widely seen as being against the rules? To put the quandary somewhat differently, is it an offense to play by anyone's rules in order to gain and to share a deeper understanding of a particular culture in relation to others? It is a hoary question for every anthropologist, but Vámbéry was not an anthropologist in the contemporary sense. He possessed, as already noted, a larger civilizational mission.

So, what really was the difference between allowing people to say one had converted to Protestantism in order to contrive a university post and allowing other people to say one had become a pious dervish in order to travel in safety? What, in other words, really was wrong with modern self-reinvention, if in fact it was simply the realization and professionalized rendition of a process that had taken place universally for many centuries? If people calling themselves Magyars could migrate to the West and become Europeans, then what really was so wrong with being an Orientalist? No—there is, and always was, one Eurasia home to multiple civilizations whose interactions and movements determine the history of every people connected to it. Sometimes it takes an intrepid autodidact like Vámbéry to reaffirm the obvious.

Fame was another matter. It carried its own penalties. Vámbéry knew it would lead to comparisons to Louis Kossuth. He may have welcomed them. But Kossuth's international fame rested on veneration in his homeland; Vámbéry sought fame outside Hungary partly in order to compensate for the lack of honors he received inside it. The distinction falls short of an antithesis, but it serves to emphasize once again that influence must, on some level, be political. From a twenty-first century point of view, Vámbéry, for all his obsession with ethnography, is regarded more as an internationalist than as a nationalist. In his internationalism, too, he influenced many followers.

4. The Mole
JAMES ANGLETON

His middle name, which he never used, was Jesus. It was presumably given to him by his Mexican mother. His father was also called James. Angleton was born in Idaho and had grown up in Italy, where his father oversaw the National Cash Register franchise, and in Britain, where he was schooled. He returned to Italy during the war, where he began his career in counterintelligence, and remained there firming up intelligence "relationships" for the Cold War, which included fixing the 1948 Italian elections to keep the Communists from taking power.

Angleton was exceedingly intelligent. He liked to keep that intelligence, and much else, carefully hidden. It was not obvious why. Perhaps he cherished or relished privacy. Perhaps he had become too accustomed to it and its advantages from his youth and the war. Perhaps he was subject to some great fear. Perhaps he had a great ambition which would fail if prematurely exposed. Perhaps he didn't much like other people.

Before his cover was dramatically blown in the 1970s, not many people had known of Angleton. It is hard to prove that he had much influence at all, but he had great power in the form of an iron veto. Angleton created and dominated for more than two decades the counterintelligence service of the Central Intelligence Agency. He had the power to end a career on the slightest suspicion, and he ended many. It is also alleged that he ended a number of lives as well, notably those of Soviet defectors whom Angleton suspected of fakery. Sent back to the Soviet Union, they were rarely heard from again.

This negative form of power is not to be underestimated, but Angleton's significance beyond his years in power is less understood and therefore neglected. It had more to do with power per se than with authority over the judgment of the powerful. To plant the most extreme suspicion permanently in the mind of officialdom writ large—one of Angleton's duties was to oversee liaison between the CIA and other intelligence agencies—is to affect their future lives. It was not only that Angleton converted a few people to his way of thinking. He also inspired others to detest it, and to denounce the terrible damage they claim he had done. For nobody after Angleton could be too suspicious, or suspicious enough.

There have been several books written about or heavily featuring Angleton, and also a number of depictions on film. Because it is most likely impossible to gain sufficient access to the documents and other historical evidence that would be necessary to reconstruct an accurate picture of either the man or his career, a true history most likely never will be written. He is the rich subject instead of popular myth, from his alleged role in covering up the details of the Kennedy assassination to the far-fetched case for his alleged Soviet loyalty. It is not surprising then that one of the best accounts of Angleton's career is one of the first and is purportedly fictional. Aaron Latham's *Orchids for Mother* uses the metaphor of the man who raises prized orchids, which Angleton was in real life, as it happens, to explain his worldview and the ways he cultivated it in the minds of other people. The first and most obvious aspect to mention is that prize orchids take a very, very long time to appear.

There was a hierarchy to Angleton's liaison relationships. The one with the Israelis was probably the closest because it was Angleton's exclusive purview. But the one with the British was probably the most consequential, because it was the oldest and the most damaging. Angleton, as already noted, was educated in a British public school, Malvern. There he got a particular education in, and from, a particular sort of person. An over-tall, awkward, bookish, half-Mexican Idahoan is not usually one who would be expected to be that sort of person, but by most accounts, Angleton did very well at Malvern and, by his account, mastered the ways of the British ruling class, their language, codes, signals.

Thus many people, Angleton probably chief among them, were surprised at how easily he had been conned by the notorious spy Kim Philby. The Anglo-American espionage relationship was extremely close during the war, and both men were in the thick of it. Philby later was posted to Washington, and took charge of seeing to British interests and liaison activities there. Well, not, as we now know, exactly. Philby was a Soviet spy, recruited in the 1930s, and part of a now notorious gang, called the Cambridge Five. Angleton had been one of his closest collaborators; the two told each other many things, perhaps, according to Angleton, nearly everything, as even today allied services say they sometimes do. And one by one all the operations about which Philby had learned were compromised; agents and operatives killed; assets lost.

The betrayal, once discovered after Philby fled to Moscow, had a visible effect on Angleton. His alcoholism worsened. So did his weirdness. The one person he ostensibly trusted, or at least the one in his business he ostensibly understood, had stabbed him in the back. He became even more secretive. Colleagues said he took to working only at odd hours in the dark with only a small desk lamp for illumination; he chain smoked; his thoughts and words sounded more conspiratorial, illogical, fantastical.

Still, his bosses at the CIA remained loyal. Angleton's reputation as a wartime legend helped. So did his own mastery of the arcane subject of counterintelligence. He had a gift for spotting patterns, patterns so obscure that understanding them happened more emotionally than intellectually. As a later director of Central

Intelligence put it, talking with Angleton was like talking with an impressionist painting. These impressions were dangerous. For nothing puts fear into the heart of an intelligence service than the prospect of being compromised from within.

Operatives trust nobody by nature; but survival forces them to trust their own. The job of counterintelligence is never to trust, but if trust is necessary, then to verify by forcing people to prove the impossible, which is to say, their own unfalsifiability.

The Cold War was suited to such twisted trees of dialectics. So was Angleton. At a minimum they protected and shielded him, for he kept, he said, the most secret secrets. At a maximum, they put his institution, his government, his integrity and honor—deep in their most protected heart—to rot. Paranoia does this to a person and to a regime. In that respect, turning Angleton paranoid was Philby's greatest success.

Philby was not alone. One day a Soviet defector called Anatoliy Golitsyn appeared. Golitsyn's method was simple, and, with Angleton, remarkably effective. Golitsyn somehow had persuaded Angleton that he was both genuine and extremely well informed. Any subsequent defector then had to pass Golitsyn's muster: If Golitsyn said he too was genuine, then he was; if not, then he was branded a double agent and sent back to his death.

Naturally there were people who said Golitsyn and even Angleton were the real double agents. But the accusation, evidently, was impossible to prove. Thus most of the period literature has fallen down a rabbit hole of psychobabble, of double, triple, quadruple agency, of mirrors and fog, and all the other usual images. What sort of game was this, really? Was Golitsyn, about whom very little is really known, the professional reincarnation of Philby? Or just a convenient crutch for a paranoid alcoholic, who also happened to wield great power over both personal and professional lives?

For Angleton it all came crashing down rather quickly, not much later. The Vietnam War and then the Watergate scandal robbed the U.S. government of its postwar reputation; scandal-mongering once again became a career maker; and secrecy of the old-fashioned sort went out of fashion. A new Director of Central Intelligence, William Colby, decided to offer up the "crown jewels" to Congress, and enumerated in public many of the clandestine (and illegal) programs the CIA had undertaken, among them several of Angleton's (for example, the effort he oversaw to open the post of U.S. citizens, not the most outrageous, to be sure, but one that recalled for many people the statement of an earlier figure who, when disbanding an earlier American intelligence service, said, "gentlemen do not read each other's mail"). The most outwardly gentlemanly of the Cold War agencies, the CIA, was rebranded an evil cabal, and James Jesus Angleton looked out his window one morning to see journalists with film cameras and microphones standing on his front lawn.

Angleton was out of a job, and a career. He died in 1987. His power had long gone. His influence is another matter.

To detect the influence of a single individual over others, as well as bureaucracies, governments, states, nations, and so on, is difficult enough. To detect a secret influence would seem impossible. In Angleton's case, it may be even more so because of the multiple layers of irony, and the easy, almost facile conclusion that the quality or even the fact of being genuine simply did not exist in his world. In reality, as it were, there was never a question of who-whom; or of which spymaster was getting one over on another; or of which bureaucracy scored the most points. It was all these things, and yet it was none of them. Nor was it a question of irrelevance: The actions of these people had deadly consequences and even, in a few cases, significant ones. The one achievement of Angleton's, for example, that's publicly known and celebrated was his acquisition through his Israeli connections of Nikita Khrushchev's secret speech denouncing Stalinism. That it became known to the world when and how it did mattered a good deal at the time. So it is not sufficient to say that so many clandestine games had little overall effect on the waging or on the outcome of the Cold War. Perhaps they did, or perhaps they did not. This is a question for historians to fight over decades and centuries from now, if they want. The question for us is, what sort of real influence did a man like Angleton have?

That question is not possible to answer without first reckoning with the modern intelligence state, or what some people like to call the intelligence community. It is vast. Nobody can say for certain how many people it employs, for in addition to numerous agencies and programs, there are thousands upon thousands of private contractors, not to mention foreign agents all around the world. In theory they all are providing some useful service, some scrap of information, some special technology, all meant to keep the world safe. For all the rest of us know, they may be succeeding in doing just that. Pearl Harbor; September 11. Just two major surprise attacks on the United States since the establishment of the modern intelligence community. The list of intelligence failures, as they're known—which include a number of policy failures where the customers of intelligence, that is to say, people in government with the job of taking decisions, chose to ignore, dismiss, or distort what intelligence officers were telling them—is longer. That is a somewhat different problem, relating as much to a surfeit of information as to willful ignorance. Most of all, it relates not to an excess but to a lack of trust.

Hence the influence of a man like Angleton. For a republic and a self-professed democracy like the United States to possess an enormous secret intelligence apparatus, and for both to function with any real degree of integrity, there must be extraordinary trust in individuals of the highest caliber. And more than that, there must be a consensus over the meaning and the exercise of trust. The man who fired Angleton, William Colby, claimed that he had no choice but to betray the existence of the crown jewels in order to regain the trust of the country and to save the CIA. It is a terrible dilemma for anyone presiding over a decadent and perversely large system, as Gorbachev-style reformers will attest. Once you let the cat out of the bag, the whole game is up. Well, that isn't exactly what happened with Gorbachev, and it certainly did not happen to the CIA. Both the Russian nomenklatura and the Agency would go on to survive (and thrive, even) under the direction of one or two more nominal reformers.

Yet, giving up the game is exactly how the people who give their lives to such organizations perceive any breach of trust, especially at the hands of the high-minded. Exactly when Angleton knew his game was up is not clear. Surely it must have come before those news cameras appeared on his front lawn. Perhaps it came the second he realized what Philby had done. Its chronology also remains a mystery.

So too will its influence. One can never know how many people were moved by the trust they placed in this man and the system he set up, and how many felt betrayed by it. Maybe it helps to recall another passion besides orchids Angleton once had: poetry. At Yale he edited a poetry magazine called *Furioso* and corresponded with some of the major poets of the mid-twentieth century, particularly Ezra Pound. His own poetry, it was said, was good enough to attract their notice and occasional praise. To work over lines of poetry in the mind over many decades, it is tempting to think, is like tending to prize orchids, silently and alone in a greenhouse that nobody sees until the moment that the flowers burst upon the world. Secrecy can have great appeal to a creative mind. To others, it can "reek of badly ventilated passions." In Angleton's case, it became deadly in ever more creative ways.

5. The Reactionary
RÉGIS DEBRAY

"Youth is wasted on the young" is the sort of tired phrase that a grandparent says to a grandchild in a moment of generational envy. It is easy to envy the young, and youth. Its stereotypes are too ingrained and difficult to dismiss from the mind. The older one gets, the more the stereotype of carefree, pretty, naïve, hopeful, malcontent youth occupy that mind. And the more they conspire in the edifice of a fashion.

For one reason or another the French are known for promoting another stereotype regarding fashion: They set it. To set a fashion means to prescribe something that is better, prettier, newer, and shinier for others to follow. The act of fashion setting therefore has as much, or more, to do with the setter than with the fashion. The French, Joseph de Maistre has written, have come to dominate the transmission of knowledge, not merely by making aspects of it fashionable, but also by universalizing the language with which it is spoken and understood. Which is to say, the French made themselves the masters, rulers, and arbiters of opinion, revolutionary opinion in particular.

The middle decades of the twentieth century culminated in the great youth revolt of 1968. It has been called the first large crack in the Cold War edifice, but it was more like a shiver: If there was a crack, it healed quickly. But the fashion of May 1968 remained strong in France and throughout the world where the youth "bulge"—all those baby boomers reaching political

40

consciousness—marched for the freedom to say and do more or less whatever they liked.

It is tempting thus to declare the youth revolt also rather tired. Revolting against their parents and grandparents, against the resentment they felt for being born when they were and for being told that they are the beneficiaries of great sacrifice; against the restrictions, as they saw them, placed upon their lives; against The System. Those are the things that young people have revolted against for as long as there were young people in the world. They start doing it at age two and eventually stop around age 35. (Or not.)

But the '68 generation had a point. Before dismissing them it is necessary to ask, just as one would do about the 1930s, where one would have stood. Who wouldn't have become a communist (or, during the thirties, a fascist)? Perhaps it was worth revolting against so many things if the world in which they were born was unnatural. This was a world dominated by European powers that had begun shedding empires in order, somehow, to remain dominant. It was a world in which dominance itself was contested, and in which a grotesque concrete wall symbolized the constructed artificiality of everything that earlier generations had by now come to take for granted. The point, then, was that thick hypocrisy was something worth revolting against.

Régis Debray was one who made revolt *qua* revolution fashionable. A son of the *haute bourgeoisie* from a Gaullist family (his mother was in politics), Debray turned sharply to the Left. In his writings and in his actions, Debray exemplified the spirit of '68 until he aged but kept fashionable as a more conventional sort of socialist and adviser to François Mitterrand. Throughout this time Debray held a strong interest in what was then called the postcolonial or Third World. In fastening it to his literary and political mode, Debray elevated the status of what might otherwise appear to be a crude form of political tourism. Yet to an extent, that is exactly what it was to those who felt his influence.

The 1960s and 1970s saw published a number of how-to guides, perhaps in prosaic homage to Mao's little red book. One of the best known was Debray's *Revolution in the Revolution*, a study and plan for socialist revolution in Latin America. It is still possible to mention it to Europeans of a certain age and hear the reply, oh, *what* a book. Latin America held a special place in the hearts of the European Left, more for what it was not than for what it was, or is, apart, of course, from the significant migration of persecuted Latin Americans who made their way to Europe during these years. It was not too foreign: Its people speak familiar European languages; its high culture, at least, looks to Europe and shares all the right references. Its politics, too, is familiar, moving along a Left-Right spectrum, and determined by the usual class, regional, and racial biases familiar to Europeans; its history includes a long period of European colonial rule, immigration, and, after independence, a number of familiar republican experiments, mostly failed. To Europeans of a certain era, saying one is the proud product of a failed Enlightenment had a certain cachet. To a twentieth century Frenchman, Latin American systems and parties— conservative/clerical, radical, liberal, socialist, and so on—would have been like putting on an old hat.

Yet Latin America is poor. Most of it, at least. And the majority of its population, and its culture, is non-European. It is a divided, hostile, and violent place. Which means that it offers the perfect laboratory for European dilettantes to—how do they put it?—*reify*.

Not only Latin America but all America was once the imagined tabula rasa for such people. They used it to invent the revolution. It was at once new and primeval; superior and pure; transformative and flagrant. How convenient then that Che Guevara, an Argentine medical doctor of mixed Spanish, Irish, and Californian descent, came along with an easy strategy to reassert the need for the New World to come to the rescue of the Old. It was called the *foco*.

The foco was a sort of incubus placed in the heart (or the belly, perhaps) of the masses that would spread revolution in all directions. It was an idea that had several antecedents, but one that Guevara claimed had succeeded in Cuba, where he became famous among the tiny group of revolutionaries that had "mobilized the peasantry" from their hideout in the Sierra Maestra in order to conquer the nation by persuasion as they defeated the enemy by arms. That wasn't quite what happened; the Cuban Revolution was won in the cities and by the widespread disaffection of the middle classes with the Batista regime; but no matter. Myths do matter, above all, in Latin America.

Debray joined Guevara in 1967 in Bolivia to establish a foco there, which would presumably spread throughout and across the Andes. That too didn't happen. Guevara was captured and killed. Debray was imprisoned. A campaign began to release him, and with the help of his prominent mother, succeeded. His fellow captor, the Argentinian artist Ciro Bustos, was less fortunate. He was a modest man who played a larger role in Guevara's operation than was known; essentially he was chief of organizing northern Argentina with an eye to its incorporation in the foco, and so had a good deal to do with logistics, supply, and recruitment. When the mission was betrayed and Guevara captured, Bustos was blamed because he was forced by his own captors to draw portraits of his fellow guerrillas. There is some evidence, however, that Debray, not Bustos, had been the one who betrayed his comrades.

In the event, Debray made his way back to France by way of Chile. Bustos eventually made his way to Sweden, the only country that would grant him sanctuary. He lived there for the rest of his life, never learning the Swedish language or exhibiting much of his artwork, though he continued to make it, as he had done in the Bolivian prison, where he sculpted chess pieces from the wooden chairs in his cell.

Debray continued to preach revolution, but remained close to the French establishment. Some people were puzzled when

François Mitterrand chose him as an adviser on foreign policy, even though Mitterrand, despite his mixed record during the Vichy period, usually got on well with other members of the Left and had succeeded in entering power with the support of the French Communist Party. Mitterrand was known for being shrewd and perhaps for being sublime as well. If he meant for Debray to serve as his emissary to the revolutionary Left, the appointment made sense; but it was more likely that the revolutionary Left, if it still exerted much influence at all (over French foreign, or any other, policy), was Debray's ambassador to Mitterrand. He continued to press for positive attention to the Third World, but he also encouraged yet another third direction for France, and for Europe more generally (albeit less faithfully), as an important repository of resistance and independence from U.S. and Soviet influence alike.

It remains for us to understand the appeal, and therefore the influence, of *tiers-mondisme*. It would be easy to call it a form of slumming, full stop. But of course it is more complicated than that. Does radical chic establish a language of influence? Or is it merely a pose?

There are several possible impulses and motivations for adopting an affinity and interest in what today is called the Global South. Certainly there may be a genuine interest in such places, not for pertaining to a geopolitical and cultural category, but for their inherent qualities. There may be a desire to redress the wrongs of the past and the present: Debray and his ilk, in that regard, were crusaders against a legion of injustices. There may be a passion for novelty: The Cold War in Europe was in style in the 1950s, with a nod to Northeast Asia; but the 1960s brought into mode a succession of newly independent states, nearly all south of the Equator. If they brought headlines, they bought careers for young (and not-so-young) upstarts in government or corporate bureaucracies, newsrooms, academic departments, and party organizations. They made aging and other would-be revolutionaries also feel young. Nikita Khrushchev succumbed and gave Fidel Castro a bear hug.

Tiers-mondisme has had a good, long run, all things considered. Many if not most of the Third World states touted by the *jeunesse dorée* of the 1960s fell soon after they rose. Most kept their sovereignty, but few became independent of the domination of international capital, commodity markets, and thieving political classes. So, the crusade against injustice continues on behalf of the Global South, and *tiers-mondisme*, minus some of the Red elements (as the one-time Communist champions of the Third World, the Chinese, have beaten the capitalists at their own game), is alive and well. So, too, for that matter, have some of the best-known '68-ers: Dany le Rouge (a.k.a. Daniel Cohn-Bendit), Bernard-Henri Lévy, Régis Debray. Their crusades continue on behalf of the maligned, persecuted, and downtrodden, as well as the imperiled natural environment.

It's easy to caricature the revolutionary type who does well by doing good. And to be fair, when many of them were marching through the streets of Paris, Debray was sitting in a Bolivian prison. Did he not have the courage of his convictions? It's hard to say he didn't. Yet few of those convictions were original. *Épater le bourgeois* has been around since the bourgeoisie first established itself. What makes such antipathy so tempting, so easy, so repetitively and predictably fashionable for the young daughters and sons of the middle class? Does being in the middle force an obsession with gradations and distinctions? Does it promote self-hatred? Does it inevitably insert a tone of apology into an accent or writing style, and the more polished the accent or style, the more subtle, and the more pronounced, the tone?

Conventional histories suggest that the French gave the world both modern, universalistic ideology and the modern class system. Others—the British and the Americans and the Russians, for example—took them to a perverse extreme, in nominally opposite directions. It was to be expected then that a Frenchman should gain fame in an attempt to undo them by discovering for himself an alternative New World; to pursue revolution in the literal sense, by going full circle back to the time when the hated middle class first made its appearance in the West and to bury it in a new state of nature; rather, to plant a new seed there. Or perhaps this is reading too much into Régis Debray.

In retrospect, *How Tasty Was My Little Frenchman* is the phrase he most brings to mind. This was the title of a Brazilian film from the 1970s in which a French captive in the South American jungle, desperate to prove he isn't Portuguese, appears for a time to go native. As the title suggests, he didn't succeed.

Loose allegories aside, Debray's story offers a good illustration of the difference between influence and inspiration. True *inspirateurs* succeed in the carnival of emotions. Influencers, some appearances notwithstanding, work through the intellect. Jesus, Marx, Lenin inspired. Paul, Engels, and Trotsky influenced. Disciples it is said are masters in the art of validation. That is true even when they depart from the line of the teacher, inventing a bit along the way. This is part of the artistry. It is the rare influencer (see Jean Monnet, above) who also inspires, that is, who inspires by way of his influence. Debray was the opposite of this person. The more he influenced his fellow-travelers, the less he inspired. Mind, he had difficult subject matter to work with. A romantic attachment to revolution almost always dies after the first shots are fired, or when the mosquito net or the fertilizer program doesn't work. Which is all the more reason to grant Régis Debray just a slight nod of appreciation. He persisted, in his own typical way, giving the bourgeois revolutionary another few lives so that somebody, somewhere has someone to upset.

6. The Architect
MIRIAM CAMPS

The first impression of her face is earnestness. The eyes convey intelligence, and the mouth just the slightest hint of curiosity. But the rest of the face, from its bone structure to its gaze to its straight angle, all say the same thing: Here is a serious woman.

The period just after the Second World War, when she went to Europe as one of the group of economists who administered the Marshall Plan, was a serious time. But serious in a different, more contingent, way. It mattered, and so did the men and the few women who went there, young Americans with a charge to tell old Europeans how to run things in their destroyed continent. Serious in being of great consequence, so it seemed; but not serious in the dire sense of the term; that is, not frightening.

Her surname then was Camp, without the "s," which was added later upon her marriage to a British academic called Tony Camps. Several of the other Marshall Planners came from academia, but she had joined the U.S. government nearly just out of Mt. Holyoke and Bryn Mawr. Their *esprit de corps* was less innocent, less experimental-minded than the eggheads who populated the New Deal programs half a generation earlier. Camps' generation was harder; it had survived the Depression and the war and had yet to be christened "the greatest," which meant that it may still have felt it had something to prove, or at least something very important to do. In her case, that something was to rescue Europe.

47

Camps came to this view over time through various wartime and early postwar official assignments. During the war she served on the Advisory Commission to the Council of National Defense and in the Office of Price Administration, and then joined the Bureau of Economic Warfare where she continued to set commodity prices and study consumer behavior. From there she moved to the State Department and to the London embassy in 1943, where she remained until 1947 as the chief economic officer in charge of the Economic Commission for Europe. She returned to the State Department in Washington that year to oversee efforts in the State Department on that and then on the Marshall Plan and other subjects related to European integration.

Anyone who knew something about the Marshall Plan knew that it had a very simple basis. It was not a giant aid program; nor was it a self-interested investment in a giant market for American postwar economic growth. It is usually depicted as both of those things, and so there is some truth in them, but the main purpose and design of the Marshall Plan came from the need to inspire confidence. The confidence necessary to rebuild economies and societies that had not seen so much destruction in many centuries; necessary to place a bet on a better, less bloody future; necessary to persuade the folks back home—the ones whose taxes were paying for all this—that all their own sacrifice in the war had been worth something. Again, that something was a new Europe designed so that this terrible war really would be the war to end all war, in Western Europe, at least.

The theory behind the Marshall Plan did not restrict itself to a particular geography, at least not in name. It was open to anyone, including to the Soviets, who surprised nobody by rejecting the offer and forcing their new satellites, after a hiccup with Czechoslovakia, to do the same. But rebuilding Western Europe was plenty enough. To inspire the right degree of confidence, the Marshall Planners had to make a point of deferring to European politicians.

We won't insist on telling you how to spend the money, the Americans said, but we'll be right here, in each country, with a "mission" to advise on the best ways we think you should spend it. If there ever were a handbook of influence-peddling, the Marshall Plan would have a prominent place. Some historians have questioned how much the Plan directly brought about *Les Trentes Glorieuses*, that remarkable period of Western European prosperity lasting until the 1970s. But one way or another, that Western Europe regained its confidence and its prosperity in record time is a historical fact.

The first priority for the recovery of the European economy was collective: Each government had to consider the position of the others, and had to coordinate policies as best they could. Some Europeans had long pushed to unite, and a big push would come soon with the establishment of the European Coal and Steel Community, an effort that would have almost surely been stillborn had it not been for the Marshall Plan and the presence of earnest Americans working side by side, as we have already read in the portrait of Jean Monnet, with the founders of the European movement. Miriam Camps did not really like the word "unification," however. It sounded too loaded. She preferred "integration." Whether or not she can really be credited as the author of this phase of "European integration," it is a nice term that has lasted a while, all things considered.

She came from a New England family descended from ministers. She grew up in Middletown, the daughter of a mathematics professor at Wesleyan. Secretary of State Dean Acheson, son of the Episcopal bishop of Connecticut and also from Middletown, got on well with her and continued to solicit her thoughts for many years. Camps didn't think their common origins mattered and doubted whether Acheson even knew of them, but she appreciated the attention.

Her job was to fit together the actual, potential, and possible pieces of European integration into a pattern of growth, which is to say, Europe needed its prosperity back, but with a different system and a different division of labor among, rather than between, national industries. Figuring out how to do that has been a contested process lasting decades, and it continues; and it was up mainly to Europeans to figure out, starting with coal and steel back in 1950. Camp and her colleagues, in the Marshall Plan, the Economic Commission for Europe, and then in the Organization for European Economic Cooperation (and later back again in the U.S. State Department), had to figure out something else, related but different. First, she had to ask the right questions.

How should European integration occur in a way complementary to transatlantic integration? How can the interests and policies of a European Community be harmonized with those of an Atlantic Community (a term once very much in vogue)? And not only economically, but also politically, and, after the establishment of NATO, militarily? Her mission was not to harmonize what are called "pol-mil" (political-military) relationships, but instead political and economic institutions and policies, with those other relationships in the background. In other words, how should the North American and the European members of the North Atlantic Alliance and emerging Atlantic Community coordinate and collaborate toward their mutual prosperity rather than compete as and among new blocs? All that was much more complicated and difficult than it sounds.

Too complicated and difficult, in fact, to elaborate here. What was first needed before slaying all the devils in the details, Camp argued, was a principle. The principle was one of organization, or what today we call global governance, by way of fortuitous duplication. That was the only way she believed it was possible to see national, regional, and global organization, and therefore, loyalties, working together rather than at cross-purposes, which had been the case up to that point in Europe, and elsewhere.

The trick to understanding it was to see, like her own surname, the handy evolution of various acronyms standing for institutions, inter alia: EEE, ECO, ECITO, ECE, ECA, OEEC, OECD, EFTA, EEC. There was no inherent problem with having multiple, overlapping or successive institutions playing similar roles, but it was better that their memberships, rather than their defined roles, rhymed and overlapped and enveloped one another, as her friend William Diebold put it, as a sort of onion. Overlapping memberships meant a rather unusual division of labor as well. National governments could play off one another in separate but related institutions, as well as trade off one another's interests; the same could occur within and across nations among different interest groups: industry, labor, etc. But the overall duplication of institutions had to bring stability, or the whole house would come crashing down. Such stools and their legs (Common Market, the Commonwealth, and the "special relationship" with the United States), as Camps once said with regard to the UK, can be wobbly. Wobbly stools need glue, as well as a strong, supporting hand now and then.

For all that a few generations of political scientists have made careers explaining an invisible hand governing such cross-institutional hullabaloo with arcane concepts like the Pareto optimum. Camps understood at the outset that the hand could not be too invisible. Rather it had to be there, "on the ground," as journalists like to say, holding the hands of like-minded Europeans, tending to their problems, and, yes, minding their confidence, which took some time to recover, probably longer than most people, even today, would admit. For her, the minding was almost always cautious, thoughtful, and faithful to the belief that it is better to keep silent about something one opposes and keep the opponents of your worldview guessing than to open your mouth and remove all hindering doubt. The language she elicited from like-minded colleagues was almost always of such a prudent nature: Let a "situation mov[e] naturally in this direction without either bringing it on too fast or posing difficult questions prematurely. Keep an eye on the evolving talk about new strategic doctrine—this is the matter that will require the most delicate handling and where we can use all the help we can get from people ... who know where the nerve endings are...."

By 1958 the Europeans had established the Common Market and were on the way to integrating much more than their economies. By now Camps had married and left government service, and had recast her career as a writer and scholar. She wrote for *The Economist* and authored one of the better books on the difficult relationship between the United Kingdom and the European Community. She continued to be a mainstay of transatlantic wisdom in some of the usual places: Princeton, the Council on Foreign Relations, Chatham House, etc. She would return to the State Department one more time in the late 1960s, toward the end of the Johnson administration, to become the first female vice chair of the Policy Planning Staff, where she remained for about two years, into the Nixon administration.

The essence of Miriam Camps' influence is less in its presumed shapeshifting movement between and among organizations, otherwise known as the Establishment's revolving door and today the semi-official norm, than in its self-conscious undetectability. Her colleagues in the State Department liked to call it the art of the light touch. The artist was not a single person but a system or norm that meant an anonymous, strategically-placed bureaucrat with certain principles, a strong will, and a deft personality could exert an awful lot of influence on small, specific policies that in turn would set all sorts of precedents or create the possibilities for greater action within a growing and ever more confident multinational regime. There were a number of such people who, like Camps, left only a few indications of their presence in various official archives, the people who just happened to be in the room, blue pencil in hand, as this or that critical clause in a treaty was drafted, or this or that critical calculation of a subsidy or tariff level was made. Upon meeting them there in dusty archival boxes, it's tough for the sentimental historian not to fall in love with them, their achievement, and, above all, their modesty. For her part, Camps liked to say that the OEEC had many fathers but only one mother. We might go a step further and call her the quiet, earnest American at the core of one of the most ambitious and, on balance, successful, political and socioeconomic experiments of the modern era.

7. The Vicar
RUSSELL LEFFINGWELL

Does an economy, a nation, a society, an empire, not need proper guardians of the private interest? Does it not need shrewd and responsible stewards of the public purse? Ask any great financier these questions and the answer will be, yes, of course, they do. Usually quietly said, with the hint of a smile. Perhaps followed by a further definition: that whoever performs these roles in public or in private are great servants of the nation, and in possession of great knowledge about that nation's position in the greater economic world. And thus whoever writes the history of the decline and fall of any nation's elite must study them.

The financier is one of the more defined stock characters. Part gray eminence, part puppeteer, part sage, part prophet, part consigliere, part guttersnipe. Often, in some way or another, faceless. Yet this is not usually or entirely, or sometimes not at all, how financiers describe themselves.

The best financiers are skillful at making displays of astuteness without appearing cynical. It is easy to admit that some have been rather good at the job—the job being not only to make money but also to convince the rest of us that they possess special powers, skills, wisdom, and knowledge—and the sense of responsibility to use them all well, no matter how many times the economy goes belly up. As soon as prosperity returns, they are feted again, with epithets like "the committee to save the world," "the masters of the universe," the "sublime oracles," and so on.

The stock character of the financier dates back to the money-changers in the Temple, gained a shine with the Medici and other Early Modern banking dynasties, but it acquired a special economy of scale in the nineteenth and twentieth centuries as private financial networks and the banks that underwrote them enjoyed a global status. Particular families or houses had become multinational enterprises.

The power of wealth being what it is, such a reputation for omnipotence is more caricature than faithful to the stock character of the financier. Great banking houses have real power, to be sure, but it is rarely limited to the individual, and is usually exceeded by their influence upon economies and therefore also upon statecraft.

One of the first instructions financiers give is to avoid unwanted publicity. For that reason many of them are not very well known. Some are almost totally unknown to posterity, except within a small circle. One such American was Russell Leffingwell. He was one of the most influential banker-servants in America of the middle twentieth century. Presidents from Woodrow Wilson to Dwight Eisenhower sometimes ignored his advice, but they listened to it. And what advice it was: remarkably shrewd, independent, prescient, witty, thoughtful, iconoclastic, humorous, and, at the same time, conventional, conservative, and almost always sensible.

Leffingwell was said to be the only partner of the House of Morgan to predict the Great Crash in 1929. He is the only one of a trio of legendary Morgan partners—the other two members being Dwight Morrow and Thomas Lamont—to lack a biography or memoir. He did not attract much attention or controversy. He was a supporter of the Democratic Party. He was, so to speak, an outlier among his ilk.

He had one or two operational gifts, foresight and discretion being the most apparent. They made him a fine banker. But he was more than a banker; or rather, he was an older breed of banker who was also ahead of his time. That combination is based on the singular distinction between private and public interests, which has long been an obsession of political theorists. American public life, or the public sector, has ascribed to the Enlightenment axiom that the sum of private interests, no matter how solipsistic or self-ish, constitutes a viable public interest through checks, balances, and other cumulative benefits. Greed is good, the interests tame the passions, the business of America is business, and so on. Leffin-gwell did not denounce that axiom, or aim to diminish it. As Dorothy Thompson once wrote to Thomas Lamont: "I didn't in the least mean to imply that Mr. Leffingwell represented vested in-terests. On the contrary, I think Mr. Leffingwell represents disin-terested intelligence. At any rate, I find that I agree with almost everything I hear of or by Mr. Leffingwell, which, I suppose, is the common definition of intelligence in others."

Yet, starting with public versus private, the axiom has thrived on binary distinctions. Many of them, such as Wall Street versus Main Street, conflate distinction with separation in the minds of many people. In coming to believe that the two are different places, with different interests, one tends to believe not only that one ought to have a certain power over the other but that, at the same time, Leffingwell's two worlds exist in separate realms of loyalty. It is absurd, obviously, to ignore the interdependent relationship of the two realms, if they really are realms. But in a legal-institutional culture such as America, which emphasizes to so great an extent the role of adversarial relations and the freedom to accumulate, that is not hard to do.

As his name and its Connecticut origins suggest, Leffingwell came from colonial stock. His paternal family settled their land there in the mid-seventeenth century; his mother was a Cornell from New York. Leffingwell was born in New York City, grew up in the Hudson Valley, and settled on Long Island. He remained in this corner of the country for the rest of his life.

Leffingwell entered banking from the law and government service, with a bit of help. His neighbor had been Woodrow Wilson's son-in-law, William McAdoo, who also happened to be the Secretary of the Treasury. Upon the suggestion of Leffingwell's colleague, Paul Cravath, McAdoo persuaded Leffingwell to abandon plans to serve as a reserve army officer and instead hired him as the assistant secretary to oversee financing the First World War. From there Leffingwell migrated back to Wall Street, eventually to the House of Morgan, where he spent the rest of his career as a partner, and as chairman from 1948 to 1950. He also chaired the Carnegie Corporation of New York, and, from 1946 to 1953, the Council on Foreign Relations, which he had helped establish. He was a member of the Century, Chevy Chase, Down Town, Knickerbocker, Metropolitan (D.C.), New York Yacht, Pilgrims, Piping Rock, Seawanhaka Corinthian Yacht, University, and Yale Clubs.

If that biographical résumé reads familiar, it should not be surprising. It's more or less identical to that of most members of the mid-twentieth century Eastern Establishment that predominated along the Boston-Washington axis, with satellites in San Francisco, Chicago, London, and a few other places in between. The men and women who were part of and party to it were a dime a dozen, and so was their influence, which was also considerable.

The term Eastern Establishment wasn't used much until the postwar decades, and the contemporary meaning of the term dates to that period, or really to the Second World War itself, when rich, powerful men and their wives set aside private pursuits to serve their country, as Leffingwell had done during the previous war. The Boston-Washington axis directed a southerly movement: Scientists, lawyers, and other intellects joined a large contingent of Wall Street bankers and headed to the nation's capital to do their patriotic duty, both in and out of public office. Many of them remained in one form or another until the 1980s, occupying roles not only in government but in its many appendages: lobby groups, professional associations, research organizations, etc.

Even if he shared a résumé with several others, Leffingwell's influence was remarkable simply because he did it before they did, laying a path and setting an example. He was a wise man's wise man.

The financier as wise man's wise man is a part of the stock image known to most students of empire, but was less familiar to Americans of Leffingwell's generation. Apart from some notable exceptions, the founders of the American republic and their progeny kept a nominal distance from the stereotypically European world of high finance. The nation's independent finances may have been necessary for its survival, as even Thomas Jefferson came to realize, but political necessity kept financial dealings at arm's length, except when they became a handy scapegoat around election time. The idea of Wall Street as existing apart from the rest of the country's politics lasted until—or culminated in, some would say—the early part of the twentieth century, and to some extent persists.

What made Leffingwell's generation of Wall Street men distinct was their having arrived to office just after the Populist and Progressive movements had done their damage to Wall Street's reputation, and, at the same time, after Wall Street had begun its remarkable rise to world power. Their relationships crossed as many borders as their minds and interests extended to areas beyond banking: the arts and, of course, politics. They were what we now call generalists, applying their wisdom and intelligence to many areas of private and public life, not to mention most areas of banking and finance. They thought and acted more deeply, and more widely, cultivated this kind of versatility, and did so for the most part without falling into the superficial weeds.

It is not surprising then that the Wall Street men, like later Davos men and women, applied to themselves a thick patina of altruism. If the business of America really was business, then the purveyors of capital had a particular responsibility to also be the stewards of economic and social order. Historians have applied additional titles to this group: financial missionaries; financial diplomats; monetary priesthood. Leffingwell's correspondents and Leffingwell himself sometimes used such ecclesiastical language.

Leffingwell's particular sermon was about the gold standard. He preached it throughout his life. For him, sound credit and a sound currency backed by gold were the anchors of civilization. If he was the wise man's wise man, he was also the gold bug's gold bug. It was his belief that the American and British central banks had lowered interest rates excessively to fuel a credit boom which led him to predict the crash in 1929. He had been consistent in warning against such loose policies. During the First World War, despite overseeing the issuing of Liberty Bonds, he pressed for higher taxes and smaller government loans. He could be rather defensive on the subject:

> Gold never has been and never will be a cure-all. Gold never has been able and never will be able to settle a continuously adverse balance of trade and payments or adverse budgetary balance. Gold never has been and never will be able to make order out of disorder, to make peace out of war. Gold is not magic. Gold is an admirable compensating mechanism for maintaining seasonal equilibrium among currencies which are already in essential equilibrium. Gold is a thermostat which will maintain the temperature of a room at 68 degrees in zero weather provided we keep the windows shut and the furnace fire going; but with the fire out and the windows open, or in midsummer, the thermostat is useless. Gold will not take the place of political and economic peace.

Thus could Leffingwell justify his position in 1933 to endorse (and, in fact, to conspire with the columnist Walter Lippmann in prompting) the decision by Franklin Roosevelt to abandon the gold standard. He got on well with Roosevelt, whom he had got to know back in the Wilson administration (Roosevelt had also, briefly, began his career as a Wall Street lawyer). The two often corresponded, and Leffingwell acceded to Roosevelt's need to be seen to keep his public distance from Wall Street. The two occasionally disagreed, and for his part Roosevelt did not hesitate to depict Leffingwell's advice as less public-spirited than it was probably meant to be, but taking the country off the gold standard was not one of those moments. The need to do so was too great.

Leffingwell still never came around to endorsing managed currencies or Keynesianism. He carried on a polite correspondence with Keynes, but there was not much overlap in thinking between them. Leffingwell's intellectual contribution was not as an adversary of the modern welfare state but instead as a habitual doubter whose methods and judgment were refined by long experience with bonds and loans. He was doubtful about Anglo-American policy coordination and the heavy U.S. role in reconstructing European economies in the 1920s; doubtful about the Dawes Plan of 1924; doubtful about much of the New Deal; doubtful about the path Wall Street had taken toward greater professionalization, that is, specialization and fragmentation; doubtful about the capacity of his fellow guardians to uphold, defend, and nurture civic standards.

He was a doubter but not a naysayer. "There is an old saying," Leffingwell once recalled about his fellow Yale man known as Mr. Republican, "that Bob Taft is always right until he has made up his mind." Leffingwell had misgivings over the creation of the Bretton Woods institutions but put his trust in them, or rather the World Bank, once it was in the safe hands of another fellow banker and wise man, Jack McCloy. He backed the Marshall Plan and convinced a fellow banker-skeptic, Bob Lovett (soon to take office as the number two man in the State Department), to get on board with inviting the Soviet Union to participate and exploiting its refusal. He backed the decision to limit war aims in Korea. When he deemed a policy sensible, Leffingwell backed it.

It is true that Leffingwell is mostly forgotten. He was neither lionized nor demonized, and so he never became prominent in the usual American way. He played the role of a guardian, but America has no guardians in a Platonic or any other real sense. Whatever wisdom Leffingwell shared with politicians came in the tone of a supplicant. The fickle, parochial people who rule don't always respond well to whispering in the ear. Their world is loud, repetitive, immediate, transitory.

For an ear-whisperer to have influence, Leffingwell showed, he had to play that role, but it too was a thermostat. The setting of the temperature happened elsewhere: in boardrooms, salons, clubhouses, dining rooms, etc. It happened not with pearls of wisdom imparted in ears, guidebooks, or secret handshakes, but instead through simple, open comradeship and mentorship. Comrades and mentees were meant to fill in the details themselves, and to turn back occasionally, reliably, and charitably to comrades and mentors like Leffingwell for quiet, earnest approval; and to proceed with doing the same. Thus operated this man and the effective, powerful, self-confident, and short-lived elite of the American Century.

8. The Sage
BRYCE HARLOW

The first thing that people usually noticed was his height. Bryce Harlow stood 5'4, with a slight build and a bald head. Such people are known to blend in with the crowd, being almost unseen, but with Harlow it was often the opposite: He was unusual. In photographs he draws the eye to himself by looking so much different than all the others: Who is that trim, tiny, bald man lurking off to the side?

Then there were his eyes, soft, thoughtful, intense—maybe intense isn't the right word, perhaps powerful is better. Or strong. They reveal a powerful or strong or intense intelligence, as eyes sometimes do, even before the observer knows that the person is really very intelligent. For Harlow, intelligence came first. It's what made his reputation at the start. Then came, at about the same time, his enormous capacity for work. And then, dominating the other two, his integrity. Bryce Harlow was a Washington rarity who became an archetype.

Given enough time, it's possible to peg anyone to a particular tribe, however, and one finds one to fit Harlow: the Southwestern Sage. Like him, they tend to be short, bald wise men of slight stature. The best known is "Colonel" Edward House, the Texan who served Woodrow Wilson as fact finder and amanuensis, until the two fell out dramatically. There was the already mentioned Bob Lovett, also from Texas, the corporate lawyer who served Franklin Roosevelt and Harry Truman as the shrewd brain of the War and later State and

Defense Departments, and founded the U.S. Air Force. Closer to our time was an Oklahoman, Jim Woolsey, whose government and legal career mirrored Lovett's in certain ways but who also, like House, styled himself, with Rhodes and White House fellowships in his quiver, a brain in action, or what would in his day become known as the "defense intellectual," about whom more will be said in the next chapter. And there was Woolsey's nemesis, the Arizona congressman Dennis DeConcini, the man who knew everyone and everything regarding national intelligence, or so he said.

With the partial exception of Lovett, a genial hypochondriac with a dry sense of humor, the Southwestern sages were earnest workaholics, as compulsive as they were conscientious, not only about the work but also about something else that's harder to put a finger on. It would be too facile to label them typical clever boys from the provinces, determined to prove one thing or another to the ruling caste. They were driven by something else, or rather, something more.

In Harlow's case, it was an obsession with the theory and the practice of public service. Whenever asked to do something, he said yes. He asked for nothing in return. He made himself indispensable in the traditional way by doing what others did not want to do for themselves, doing it efficiently, effectively and, sometimes, brilliantly. He made himself trustworthy. Not simply because he was known to be honest and shrewd and "self-effacing" but also, and probably mainly, because he gave the impression of being fearless, willing to take political risks for the sake of the boss and the mission. His favorite line, later repeated by people who knew him (for example, George Shultz, who said it constantly; Harlow, like Jean Monnet, had a talent for planting semantic seeds) was that trust is the coin of the realm. Harlow held on to that coin as tightly as he could.

Harlow came from a family of educators and newspaper publishers in Oklahoma. He was brought up with a proximity to power, albeit provincial by today's standards. It took him to Washington, where, on the pretext of writing a thesis about the House Ways and Means Committee, he was given a job as an assistant librarian in the House of Representatives. He really did work as a librarian, although one is tempted here to think of the French sense of the term: The official "librarians" are almost all spies. So, too, in Harlow's case: As assistant librarian he had so little to do that he spent most of his time observing, taking notes, working on his thesis, etc. But the experience laid for him an important foundation, and was memorable in more ways than one. Another assistant librarian hanged himself after losing his patron, and therefore his job.

During the war, he joined General Marshall's staff, followed by a return to the Hill as a staffer on the House Armed Services Committee. He took to that, too. He became its chief of staff in 1948. From then on his special expertise, the one that people turned to over and again, was the heart and mind of the Hill. He had a gift for understanding them. How committees and subcommittees worked. How all the sausage making and horse trading was done. How persistence—that underrated quality, as we have already seen, that the best influencers have—also worked and how much it mattered. And how to make oneself useful, needed, and wanted by the fickle and bloody-minded people in power.

These gifts and acquired talents took Harlow to the White House in 1952. President Eisenhower saw another gift and talent: Harlow could write. That was saying a lot, for Eisenhower himself had risen through the ranks of the interwar army as a staffer who wrote speeches, for General Douglas D. MacArthur, no less. Harlow had a way with words and also, just as important, a capacity to see a situation, a problem, or a necessity through the eyes of the other guy, as Ike liked to say. To say that capacity appealed to the president would be an understatement. This president admired Harlow's capacity for empathy, which matched his own to the point of ventriloquism. He loved it, and the idea of it. And he loved Harlow and his speeches.

By these qualities and his usual hard work, Harlow became Ike's indispensable man of words and his Congressional liaison. By default he also became the young wise man of party politics, the president's ambassador to Congressional Democrats, especially to Senate Majority Leader Lyndon Johnson, with whom, after a couple of early bumps, Harlow got on very well; and the de facto legislative manager, packager, and, to an extent, chief intellectual of what would be, despite some appearances, two underappreciated and rather successful administrations.

The work left him exhausted, often dispirited, but never bitter or angry; or he never showed that it did. The showing was part of the wielding of influence: Never let them see you down. It fit well with the optimistic ethos of the administration. Humble yes; sardonic, sometimes; down, never. Keep working; keep thinking; keep writing and rewriting; keep making yourself useful; keep being the outwardly honest broker; keep being wise and tactful.

But eight years of this slog was enough. Out went the Republicans in 1960, and out went Harlow. Or, by some measure, he went up, following Secretary of Defense Neil McElroy to (or, in the case of the latter, back to) Procter & Gamble. Harlow became its Washington representative: in other words, a lobbyist. And here too he acquired a new label: pioneer. He dressed influence-peddling in a gray flannel suit so well that it no longer seemed like influence-peddling at all, but instead an auxiliary to public service. He established the Business-Government Relations Council, a group of public-spirited, public-minded people like himself, still trying their best to be useful to those in power. They did not claim to be disinterested; they were not hypocrites, and trust remained the coin of the realm. What Harlow did was to establish K Street, as we know it today, as its own brand, as not only a lobbying industry but also a quasi-official arm of the state, an organic part of the body politic whose separation from policy-making would now be inconceivable.

When Richard Nixon returned to the White House in 1969, he summoned Harlow back to official service as his second presidential appointment, following that of his long-time secretary, Rose Mary Woods. He must have known Harlow would not say no, although it is hard to believe that his heart was in it. He liked being a lobbyist: better hours, less publicity, more money. But when a president asks ... yes, one must say yes.

Harlow's duties to Nixon were different from those he performed for Eisenhower but not entirely unique. He would again serve as chief Congressional liaison and, in that role, as a political sounding board and booster for the administration's policies; as an originator of, among other things, Nixon's Southern strategy; but in this instance there was an additional, more burdensome duty, which was to supervise or mitigate, as best he could, the rough elbows of Nixon's principal councilors: John Ehrlichman, Robert Haldeman, and Chuck Colson.

Harlow failed in that final duty, and the blame rests mainly with Nixon, who liked and indulged the roughest of elbows. But the failure also illustrates the limit of Harlow's influence. It flourished among like-minded people; it refined, advanced, and perfected policies and beliefs that were already in place; it served to deflect and occasionally to isolate opposition to them rather than to persuade such opposition to change its mind. That is not to say that Harlow's brand of influence could not be persuasive, but rather that it came from a sort of tactical persuasion that Harlow identified as hermaphroditic: Come on side and your side will be momentarily better off. Anything more fundamental—a strategic shift in political direction, for example—was better left to the bosses, or, better yet, to the people.

It is one of Washington's truisms, and it may be true in other capitals as well, that the people who make it are those whose tactical dexterity and willpower are infinite but whose strategic imagination is conventional and even myopic. That was certainly the case with the chief survivor of the Nixonian implosion, Henry Kissinger, who, in addition to having an extremely keen sense of public image, also had a beautiful sense of timing. (He was also complimentary in his memoirs toward Harlow, though one of his first acts in office was to steal Harlow's private West Wing washroom). But none of the great strategic decisions for which Kissinger has taken credit—the opening to China, the expulsion of the Soviets from the Middle East, the transformation of European détente into an ending of the Cold War—originated with him. In fact, he opposed nearly all of them at the outset, on very sensible tactical grounds. But when ordered to march, he marched, and devised the brilliant tactics that brought them home.

Harlow lacked that sort of ambition and disdained that sort of deviousness. The Watergate scandal put an end to his career as an honorable courtier. He had nothing to do with enacting the scandal, but froze when he was lied to by the president at the moment when he found that he could do almost nothing to limit the damage. About the only service he could pull off, which preceded the Watergate crisis, was to succeed in having Gerald Ford replace Spiro Agnew as vice president once Agnew had been tarred with the brush of corruption, which was ironic, as Harlow had been one of Agnew's most loyal supporters. Loyal, more or less, to the end.

What is the role of a sage in a democracy? What is the nature of sagacious influence? What is its import? Kissinger, who helped make "realism" a household term, described in his usual perceptive way Harlow's influence as follows:

> Today's rulers have most of the problems Machiavelli wrote about, but in particular, they can ill afford any confusion between appearances and reality. To guard

against such confusion, every great leader requires the services of a few trusted advisors. When we wish to be unkind, we refer to them as Machiavellis. When we wish to be generous, they are known as Elder Statesmen. No matter ... it is all the same. Such individuals must possess a special gift to find reality among conflicting points of view and a special kind of relationship to the leader they serve.... The names of national leaders [Harlow] served have become legendary in the history of the Republic. If each were able to pen a foreword for this history they would write that those legends were created in part by the sturdy fabric of reality woven day by day by Bryce Harlow.

It is not enough to call these people trusted advisors or father confessors. Their worth comes not from the advice they gave, however much they may quietly be known for it, but from the influence they and that advice had at critical junctures. And at less critical ones, as well. This comes as much from tone and style as substance, and demonstrates that a reputation for sagacity can be as influential as sagacity itself. For his part, and despite vowing it more than once, Harlow never returned to Oklahoma, but spent the remainder of his days married to his second wife, his former secretary, and living modestly in a suburb of Washington, D.C.

9. The Gambler
ANDREW W. MARSHALL

The Pentagon, the headquarters of the U.S. Department of Defense, is the largest office building in the world. With more than 25,000 workers, it resembles a small city, with shopping facilities, recreation centers, "neighborhoods" of different shape, size, and character, and its own particular culture. That culture, for lack of a better term, can be described as one of conspicuous anonymity.

It is not easy to get lost in the Pentagon. The halls, the uniforms one sees along the way, the lengths one has to go to get anyplace, all in their variety look more or less the same. But the room numbering system, including floors, concentric rings, and corridors, is easy to navigate.

Andy Marshall was the epitome of the anonymous bureaucrat. His office, at 3A932, was on the inside A ring as opposed to the top officials on the outer, E ring, but was really only a short walk down the ninth corridor. An economist of medium height, bald, and very quiet, he never attracted attention in public, nor inside the Pentagon, for that matter, where the most senior officials are surrounded by aides and assistants. He was seen one evening, after rush hour, waiting in the Pentagon subway station for his train. He wore a dark suit, held a small, and not very thick case, walked softly then stopped in front of the tracks, looking straight ahead, and waited, patiently, easily, calmly.

Such a demeanor was perhaps partly responsible for his outsized reputation. For at least the last third of his very long career—

he finally retired when he was 94 years old—Marshall was known by some as the gray eminence of the American national security state. It was an odd status for a man who was almost never seen but also very rarely heard. When he did speak, he usually asked a simple, perhaps a deceptively simple, but incisive question, such as, "What is the meaning of being second?"—and almost never gave an answer.

From the small cell that he ran for four decades, called the Office of Net Assessment, Marshall was said to guide the fate of nations. None of the seven presidents or thirteen secretaries of defense he served dared fire him (one tried, meekly, and failed). By reputation, he was perhaps the most influential American defense intellectual of the twentieth century; yet only very late in his career did he and his work become known outside a tight network.

Marshall grew up in Detroit, the son of English immigrants. His father was a stonemason and his mother a house servant. During his youth he read in his local public library a great deal in many subjects, taking a special interest in the grand historical tableaux of Arnold Toynbee and the stories of Ford Madox Ford, but his most important teachers were the man who ran his school's foundry and another who ran the machine shop. He prepared first to be a manual laborer and then an engineer, and spent the war years stateside after being exempted from combat for a heart murmur. He made tools in an aircraft factory. From there he went on to study statistics and mathematics, and finally economics, at the University of Chicago as a transfer student. He took to the subject but he left before earning a PhD. On the advice of a professor, he went to California in 1949 to join a new organization set up by the Air Force called the RAND Corporation. He remained there for 25 years.

Marshall learned and perfected a number of things at RAND: how to work in small teams; how to deliver a briefing; how to persuade a superior without appearing to try; how to choose the right things to measure and how to measure them when one can almost never be certain; how to put himself in the mind of an adversary by understanding its organizational culture, its patterns of behavior, its vulnerabilities and limitations, and its habits, good, bad, and endemic; how to manipulate the weaknesses of *déformation professionnelle*; how to think and plan for events and conditions about a decade ahead; and how to judge predictions; how to mistrust rational thinking, quantification, action, and rationality; how to establish criteria for judgment, and how to test them; how to strike out in new directions. He also got rather good at playing bridge and Kriegspiel.

From RAND, Marshall went to work in the U.S. government, recruited first by Henry Kissinger and then moving to the Defense Department when his RAND colleague, friend, and fellow economist, James Schlesinger, became Secretary.

The Office of Net Assessment is small. During most of Marshall's time it had about a dozen people, mainly officers from the military services in the grade of lieutenant colonel and a few civilians. Each was responsible for determining how best to think about a specific military balance, such as NATO/Warsaw Pact, East Asia, military investments, etc. Its records are secret and probably will remain so for a long time. Thus it is not possible to know precisely how many hits and misses there were. But if Marshall had an idea, or could be provoked by an idea, he would fund it and its source and, in the manner of a venture capitalist, allow them the freedom to test themselves to any logical or illogical conclusion. The subjects of the studies he funded coincided with his diverse interests, not only in military history and strategy, but also in anthropology, biology, biomedicine, demography, management, mathematics, and philosophy.

What did he do to make himself and his office so influential? As with other successful wielders of influence, the answer comes less from what he did than from how he did it. It was not really like the method touted by William Langer, the historian who founded the analytical branch of the Office of Strategic Services (OSS, later CIA), which was that of the soldier in the trenches during the First World War: Stand up and fire in all directions with varying amounts of enthusiasm, and hope that you hit something. You sometimes did. Or you ran out of ammunition or were overrun. This was another way of describing the mixed success of Monte Carlo method of statistics Marshall specialized in at RAND. Or, as he once stated, "There are no rules of choice that are both simple and complete and agreed upon by reasonable men, but reasonable choice is possible nonetheless even in the case of uncertainty."

One or two of his ideas have become legends in their own right. The Revolution in Military Affairs, for example, is said to have defined the nature of the twenty-first century military with its emphasis on greater mobility, satellite technology, precision warfare, and so forth. The competitive strategies approach to understanding military and political rivalries forced defense planners to focus on the logic, axioms, and behavioral patterns of adversaries rather than on the usual menu of presumed intentions and partly detected capabilities. In this instance, it pitted long-term American comparative advantages against enduring Soviet weaknesses in a manner that was, at least presumably for the United States, indefinitely sustainable. Both sets of ideas were more about means than about ends. Still, Marshall's redefinition of the discipline of estimates with a multidisciplinary reorientation of strategic thought, or what he modestly called "scanning the environment," in effect amounted to a reinvention of warfare.

Reinventing warfare by aligning it with advances in technology goes back to the origins of warfare itself, but the aim here was not to reinvent for its own sake; it was, rather, to obtain with technology a qualitative advantage for dominating a battlespace in order to win battles, or ideally, to prevent them from happening in the first place. How? The answer relates to the second set of ideas and to the vague but essential quality of strategic deterrence. Marshall's contribution was to conceive and then pursue a strategy of ending the Cold War peacefully by persuading, through deterrence, the rulers of the Soviet Union that they almost certainly could never prevail against the United States and its allies and, ultimately, that they could no longer peacefully coexist in their own sphere in the manner to which they were accustomed. The reason came from its own structural, systemic, and idiosyncratic, human vulnerabilities, which Marshall's method—or rather, approach—to estimates had detected and sought to exploit.

Deterrence for him became, like the Cold War itself, less a sophisticated art than a difficult craft of signaling, of influencing the mind of an adversary so that each side might compete without resorting to nuclear war. Framed thus as an extended competition, it was informed by careful study of the mind of adversaries, their debates, intellectual passions, modus operandi, and behavioral record. Such a "strategic choice" carried with it a self-definition of superiority. The "criterion problem" involved not only superior selection but also superior diagnosis and measurement of a particular capability, weapons system, problem, asymmetry, or presumed motivation, including how to frame it, understand it, plan for it, affect it, probe it, complicate it, constrain it, exploit it, penalize it, defeat it. In assessing the pros and cons of the B-1 bomber, for example, it was important to assess the likely cost of Soviet countermeasures, presuming that the bomber would make necessary expensive and dispersed defenses. Or the development of stealth technology, which rendered Soviet strength in submarines less menacing, even fruitless. Competing in this way with the Soviet Union, no longer directly, as in a race or bout, but rather indirectly as in a judo match, meant searching for vulnerabilities, weaknesses, and gaps, as well as likely under- and over-investments, relative to one another, and to those of other powers.

Marshall's focus on Soviet vulnerabilities meant that he was prescient about the duration of Soviet power, and in predicting not the precise timing and manner of the demise of the Soviet Union but certainly the fact of it. Also, by the middle of the 1980s and then almost obsessively toward the end of his career, he anticipated the speed and determination of a rising Chinese adversary. He had a knack for getting others to pay attention to these predictions. The CIA revised its approximations of Soviet defense expenditure as a result of Marshall's work. Yet according to him, his most enduring influence, or as American bureaucrats like to say, legacy, was in the education, mentorship, and bureaucratic placement of like-minded students. The members of St. Andrew's Prep, as they are called, have sown institutional and intellectual seeds. They still hold reunions.

It is important to inquire into the nature of Marshall's influence. Apart from the ranks of Prep students and his carte blanche at the highest levels of America's national security state, there was his pattern of thought and action. He was, by most accounts, a passive, almost inscrutable, teacher and, in a way, a rather traditional don. He compared a Net Assessment to a doctoral thesis, given the amount of work put into it. As supervisor, he rarely told the writer what to do or how to do it besides setting forth the assignment. But when a draft would reach him, he tended to wrinkle his brow and say something like, "This isn't quite right." He established not a method or recipe for thinking but instead a way or logic of thinking, a habit or tendency, even, to reorient the strategic mind in a particular direction.

Such logic did not follow a set of directives or advance a firm guide to action, but rather helped and conditioned decision-makers to consider alternative types of reasoning and different questions, without having to tell them what to do to make use of tentative answers. Testing the value of questions often meant, in effect, challenging the assumptions of intelligence reports and analyses, and for that Marshall sometimes liked to make use of historical analogies: In one of his better-known commissioned studies, he asked not why France, with the best army in Europe, was defeated so easily in 1940, but instead, why Germany, with an inferior army, battlefield disadvantages, and an unenthusiastic officer corps, was so quick to seize victory. Marshall's questioning would begin with principles, which he considered easy to formulate, and then followed with their application, which was more hard going.

Why did he get things right? Predicting the bankruptcy and dissolution of the Soviet Union was not much of a guess, but it is surprising that so few people did. He also got right the relationship between twenty-first century technology and warfare, as well as the position that China would come to assume vis-à-vis his own country. None of those predictions were difficult but, again, it's remarkable how many of the best and brightest failed to make them or to believe them when they were made.

It is easy to conclude that Marshall's economical mind was just better at casting assumptions. He made as many as the next economist, but his were just better, somehow, or at least sufficiently perspicacious to appear wise, probably because they dispensed with the blanket assumption of rationality. For Marshall, habits, biases, fears, and, above all, axioms and ingrained patterns of thinking mattered most. Or maybe he benefited from the limits of Langer's method, that is, from the law of averages.

There is a third possible interpretation, however, besides asserting that Marshall had a special gift for prognostication or for chancing the odds. His gift was in his capacity for weighing probabilities, for defining risk, and for dealing with uncertainty. It started with an emphasis on diagnosis and counter-diagnosis; testing, rejecting, and re-testing assumptions. In doing so, his method emphasized the likelihood of possible dangers as much as opportunities; in truth, the two co-existed in a dialectic: The further ahead a decision-maker knew of the dangers, and of the vulnerable sources of danger, the more opportunities would exist not only to avoid danger but also to turn it back against its source. Thus the label, net assessment. A gross assessment would be little more than an inventory with a ranking. Marshall's genius for influence came from the replacement of gross with net, thereby giving those who were influenced a special, qualitative advantage in thought and, presumably, action.

Andrew Marshall was a private man. He had two wives, marrying the second late in life after the death of the first, and no children. His main interest, besides his desire for knowledge of the world and for serving his country, was French food and wine. He spent a good deal of time in France on holiday, until joining the U.S. government and doing without one for thirty years.

To sum up, as one would draft a net assessment, Andy Marshall mainly influenced in three ways, which, taken together, changed the American military mind. He redefined the concepts of risk, threat, and uncertainty from residing along a spectrum of fear to one of opportunity. He redefined the character of the Cold Warrior to be the professional defense intellectual from that of the banker, lawyer, or social scientist and part-time or amateur public servant. And he redefined the future as it is known in the present to military and other planners from a linear to an alternative reality by substituting presumed futures for predicted ones, and then focusing on their probability with the aim of mastering the conditions and the causes of their manifest power.

10: The Grammarian
MEG GREENFIELD

The editorial page of the modern American newspaper is a special, paradoxical place. It's one of the least read sections, but one of the most belabored. Editorial staffs argue interminably over single words or commas in some editorials; the page's editors and writers are second only to the diminishing breed of foreign correspondents in measuring the size of the chips in their shoulders; close behind come a newspaper's regular opinion columnists, usually appearing on the page opposite (hence op-ed), where gaining a rare guest slot can be as tough and competitive as getting your kid into a Park Avenue pre-school, or winning the lottery.

That's how it used to be, at least. In the past couple of decades, the hierarchy of print has eroded as the newspaper business itself has gone into freefall. There are easier ways to get one's ideas into circulation, although the editorial and op-ed pages of some dailies still preserve a bit of allure, if not for general readers then for some cognoscenti.

The main point of an editorial is, of course, to exert influence. Ostensibly its writer seeks to persuade a well-targeted audience of a particular viewpoint, but in the selection of topics, arguments, and evidence, and in the placement and timing of the editorial, the aim is to "set the agenda" of the day. It was once said that every government official from the third tier on up receives her or his marching orders from the front page of the major dailies, and the talking points from their editorial pages.

Meg Greenfield, the longtime head of the editorial page of the *Washington Post*, did more than nearly anyone to establish that reputation. She edited the page for twenty straight years. She did that in the usual way of an editor: setting the tone of the page, cultivating writers, polishing their prose, and the like. Yet her influence went beyond all that. She was the closest of any editor, including the famous editor-in-chief, Ben Bradlee, to the newspaper's famously insecure and later iron-willed publisher, Kay Graham. It would not be too bold to say that she was Graham's conscience and confidante, checking the punctuation and syntax in the *Post's* growing reputation as the anxious, ambitious runner-up to the *New York Times* as the nation's newspaper of record. Graham did not exaggerate when she wrote that Greenfield "helped create the institutional voice of the *Washington Post.*"

Institutions were built and others were torn down during America's own strange and rather mixed *Trente Glorieuses*. It was the *Post* that broke the Watergate story, and the *Post* that took most of the real risk in reporting it. If this newspaper with its accidental publisher, thrust into the job after the suicide of her husband, would not collapse under the pressure, it needed such a conscience, whose ethical and moral expression was as precise as it was fervent in the cause of justice. For it had to be. A good, conscientious editor will say that orthographic and other slips are more than mere distractions. They take away from the integrity of a piece, cause the reader to doubt the reliability of the author and the author's sources, and make the medium the subject instead of the message. Even the slightest exaggeration, white lie, or twisted piece of prose can ruin an otherwise excellent piece of writing. Above and beyond seeing to stylistic consistency and a well-curated diversity of coverage, the page editor must see to the details of writing with genuine and unrelenting care. He or she tends to the grammar of power.

Editorial influence is hard to get right. Greenfield's training, fortunately, was in English literature. She got it at Smith College, moving east from Seattle, where she grew up as the daughter of an antiques dealer, auctioneer, and occasional performer (her mother died very young, when Meg was eleven). After Cambridge, Rome, and Greenwich Village, she settled in Washington, D.C., where, apart from summers back in Washington State, she spent the rest of her life.

Greenfield was one of those people known as semi-public, a nebulous term appearing throughout this book which can best be described as being known by some but not by most, yet influential to many. The newspaper editorials she wrote or edited were not signed. But her sparse, clear, and literary style was certainly recognizable. They, like the old *Post* when the Grahams owned it, had a familiar and familial feel, something implicit and shared. It could be felt in its large cafeteria; when visiting it on a Sunday, one recognized some of the faces and smiled at their formal way of being informal (the image of the old dean of the political reporters, David Broder, wearing Kennedy-style short pants and long black socks, waiting patiently in the serving line, holding his tray and fumbling in his pocket for change, sticks in the mind). Perhaps this is true of most newspapers, especially the old family-owned ones (of which almost none remain), but there was something more piquant about the *Post*. It would be almost trite to say that the feel was, like its owner, at once tough and feminine. Or it could have come as much from Greenfield's quiet, assuring, shrewd eye that could "see around the corners of your mind." It was a certain attachment that one sensed, from the house style to the selection of topics. Greenfield deplored what she called the detachment of younger generations of journalists, the peddlers of what she called effigy journalism. By that she meant a misconstruing of journalistic objectivity to mean a detachment from life and from empathy with one's subjects, forcing them instead into plastic molds of easily-labeled perfection.

Her wisdom was of a more flawed, less expressive, and therefore more pragmatic, nature. Here, for instance, she makes an obvious observation that arrives gently:

> Typically, the Washington protégé must be able to offer his benefactor two delicately balanced assurances. First, he must show that he has the capacity to accomplish and a mind of his own, who will thus be perceived as a legitimate representative of his generation and not just some stooge or clone of the elders. Then too, he must show that he has no intention of going out and blowing up the power station tomorrow morning, since he aspires to inherit the thing intact.

One observation often repeated about Greenfield's city is attributed to President Harry Truman, who said, if you want a friend in Washington, get a dog. But it is not true that Washington is a friendless or unfriendly city. In Greenfield's time, certainly, and perhaps still in some ways today, it remains a big Southern town. People there smile at strangers. Few people do that in Northern cities. The smiles may sometimes be false, but they serve a purpose. You never know in Washington who may be useful. The smile, however forced, is a tiny insurance policy to put your own mind at ease, and to allow you to look over people's shoulders at receptions in case a more useful person has just entered the room.

There is a story told about Robert Gates, the Director of Central Intelligence and later Secretary of Defense, regarding one of his first assignments as a new member of the Nixon administration. His boss hated receptions and used to make Gates go in his place. Gates grew so tired of the false smiles as the people he talked to looked over his shoulder, that he decided to deploy a white lie. "Where do you work, son?" (The usual question). "I am the assistant to the deputy commissioner of Internal Revenue." (Suddenly, a direct look and a bigger smile.) "Why, it's nice to meet you."

This was Greenfield's Washington: a society of cliques, false smiles, posturing, and positioning. "What is relevant?" she asked. "What is dirty? What is fair? What is just ever so *slightly* cheap, and you know it? What is conventional wisdom and pack-pressure leading you someplace you don't really want to go but don't quite have the guts or self-assurance not to?" Yet it was not an empty, soulless city, not at all. Most of its tastemakers lived within a few blocks from one another in Georgetown or nearby. Their minds and experience were as small-town as any other, yet they were conscious, perhaps over-conscious, of living and ruling an imperial capital by half, "neither Rome nor home," as the saying went. It was not, despite appearances, a society animated principally by enmity. Friendships were everything in Washington, and Greenfield, who never married and whose only sibling, a brother, died young, was a connoisseur and dependent and protagonist of friendship in a city where even the concept of friendship was perverted, reoriented by politics, egoism, and self-interest. The culture of the *Post* drew a great deal from her friendship with Kay Graham, just as its healthy balance sheet derived from Graham's friendship with Warren Buffett. The nature of Graham's two friendships no doubt was rather different, and one need not pry too much into either (especially the latter one) to suspect with good reason that they strayed well beyond the balance sheet of the newspaper.

Such friendships, whether Platonic or something else, make possible the sort of intangible influence that several other figures in this volume were able to master. The influence was inseparable from other intangible qualities: trust, reputation, integrity, discipline, confidence, intimacy, independence, and charm. All operate differently for today's electronic influencers. That is not to say that their smile, which is to say, their appeal, is any more false than the old-fashioned kind; rather it is to emphasize its disconnection from any direct form of human attachment, that is, friendship, in the way that Greenfield and her friends understood it.

What some of them also understood was that friendship was akin to an anchor in a society that had already begun to reach a point of decadence. A leitmotif of Greenfield's writing is an awareness of that decadence, and of what she bemoaned as a steady loss of authority and erosion of standards and discipline, in the life, public as well as private, of the city she loved. She fashioned the tone of the *Post* as a bulwark against decadence, but she knew, or must have known, that it would not last for much longer. As it happens, she was also a connoisseur of potty-culture: cable news, tabloids, and late-night television, in which she indulged with not quite a morbid fascination but rather with another awareness or sensibility that these timeless pastimes of the collective ego were, again, irrepressible.

Yet, it would not be entirely fair to call Meg Greenfield a romantic. Perhaps she had once sought to be a novelist, even a romantic novelist. To even her closest friends she kept shtum on her personal life, the romantic failures that she alluded to once or twice. She may well have fallen in love with her city as a way of compensation, or not as any way at all. For there is too little that she left behind for us to read her mind and her spirit in aid of reconstructing her intellectual and emotional life for their own sake.

But for the sake of her professional life, her life's work, and the culture she "helped create" at the *Post*, which was, by most historical measures, the conscience of the city and the nation in her time, there is a plenitude. The culture as she recalled it possessed a certain mystique. And no mystique lasts. Maybe it never existed at all, except in posthumous retrospective. But retrospectives also matter. What better to romanticize than the recent past?

Meg Greenfield made romance possible in the most unromantic of imperial capitals. She may not have believed much, or for very long, in the mystique, but she edited it well. It did not sing, but it spoke—clearly, powerfully, efficiently, confidently. Like her, for a brief moment in the second half of the twentieth century, it was intelligent, honest, serious, and dignified. It also had a rather good sense of humor. It was all these things for being self-made, partly by accident, partly by design. And like her, it is today almost completely gone.

11: The Protégé
FREDERIC PROKOSCH

Literary fame is a fickle beast. Most writers know that, when going into the business, if they persist, they become either stubborn aspirants or principled dissenters. Neither stance is altogether admirable. The career of the American writer, Frederic Prokosch, demonstrates this point.

Prokosch's first book, *The Asiatics*, got a great reception when it appeared in 1935. The praise was well deserved. It is written so vividly—conflating perfectly, some might say, character with setting—that it's nearly impossible to believe the author did not directly see all the places and people he described. Yet Prokosch used entirely written sources. For the interwar youth, especially, the book gained cult status. My own copy is of Second World War vintage, printed on cheap brown paper and in a rectangular shape made to fit inside a soldier's breast pocket. This for one of the most sensual narratives in twentieth century American literature.

The Asiatics began a career for Prokosch also in conflating fact and fiction in compelling fashion. His own book of memoirs, *Voices*, or "an album of portraits," as Prokosch called it, tells of conversations with many famous people, mostly literary figures as well as royalty and other eminences, to whom Prokosch had been granted special, seemingly exclusive access. He recounts their conversations and correspondence as carefully as he had earlier painted scenes in faraway Asia. Were the memoirs truthful? It doesn't matter, really, to those reading Prokosch for the high melodrama his writing offered. Or it shouldn't. The memoirs read very well.

Prokosch was born in Wisconsin, the son of an Austrian émigré father and a Baltimore-born mother, and grew up there, in Texas, and in Chicago, after a short time in Europe. His parents were scholarly and musical. Frederic went on to earn a PhD in literature, and taught briefly at Yale and New York University. He abandoned the path of an academic career (also his father's, as it happens) and struck out on his own with commissions and grants for writing and translating, with a brief interruption during the war as an observer/attaché/propagandist for the American government in Portugal and Sweden. His writing career lasted for several more decades, but never resumed its pre-war success. Prokosch spent his final years living in southern France, almost unknown outside that country.

He had other talents as well: tennis, squash, painting, lepidopterology. And, later, forgery.

Prokosch has been the subject of a short study by Radcliffe Squires, a curious but rather unkind biography by Robert Greenfield, and somewhat kinder portraits by Pico Iyer and Gore Vidal in the *New York Review of Books*. The final one is a review of Prokosch's memoirs. "The voice one hears," Vidal writes, "is not so much his as the voices of those whom he has admired or at least listened closely to. By and large, he has chosen not to praise himself, the memoirist's usual task. Instead he has tried to distill the essence of each voice rather than what might have been exactly said."

Which stance is more egotistical for a writer? With Prokosch this question is very difficult to answer. He has described himself as fundamentally unknowable, but in nearly every poem, essay, and novel he drops a hint—of special, superior, 'profound' knowledge, intimacy, wisdom, or, as he put it, "cunning"—each covered by a mask of barely concealed plainness, even innocence.

The attitude is contrived, certainly, but to what end? It's tempting to say that it's little more than the over-exertion of a provincial, resentful at being excluded from the club but determined to be admitted nonetheless, or at least to be connected to it in some way, much as the young Prokosch used to send nude photographs of himself to writers he admired. He did not receive many grateful replies.

Vidal insinuates that the attitude, or later, the stance, was one of choice:

> He seems to have enjoyed his literary success without ever having taken on the persona of the great author. Also, surprisingly, Dr. Prokosch has never taught school; never sought prizes or foundation grants; never played at literary politics. He seems to have been more interested in the works or voices of others than in himself as a person (as opposed to himself as a writer), a characteristic that tends to put him outside contemporary American literature; and contemporary American literature, sensing this indifference to the games careerists play, extruded him entirely from the canon. He was like no one else, anyway. He had always been a kind of expatriate at a time when the drums of America First had begun to beat their somewhat ragged martial tattoo. Finally, he was dedicated to literature in a way hard for his contemporaries to grasp as they pretended to be boxers or bullfighters—not to mention bullshitters, Zelda Fitzgerald's nice phrase for the huge hollow Hemingway who had set the tone for a generation that only now is beginning to get truly lost.

This too is, as already noted, an exaggeration and falsification in most respects. So it's tempting to make a case that Prokosch's "literary" project was a great metafictional experiment. The problem was that so many people seemed to fall for it. Prokosch more likely watched his fate accumulate outside himself, not as the product of his great imagination but as the victim of it. In one of his lesser novels, *The Idols of the Cave* (1946), he offers a response of sorts in a description of another emigré, "Baron Legué":

> The baron was a collector of old glassware. Behind him stood a cabinet filled with rows of old wineglasses which he had picked up, one by one, in the antique shops of New York; fine Venetian, Bohemian, Jacobite goblets, touched with the iridescence of age. The lamplight fell on their delicate curves and tall, spiraling stems. One breath of air, it seemed, and they would fall into fragments. And the baron himself, with his frail, tapering mind, looked as brittle as his glasses; he seemed about to collapse.

Alas, not yet. Prokosch persists:

> "We've tried to build our own little Europe over here," he continued in his weary, melodious voice. "We built our pathetic replicas of Paris and Brussels, and tried to protect them from the hurricane." He fixed his bloodshot eyes on Pierre with sudden animation. "But now the war is over. Listen, my boy. The war was not precisely pleasant, but it was only a hint, a prelude to the approaching melodrama. The world has grown too small for our machinery, and too big for our hearts. All we see is stone, metal, paper, numbers, names; they've fallen like a curtain over the shape of man. We'll have an era of weird little cults, I suppose, a hysterical hodgepodge of panaceas. But they'll be useless, one and all. Just a kind of lurid rhetoric. The great new pestilence will continue.... Millions of little people are

swarming in the streets outside. But they're turning into ghosts. Their capacity for freedom is dying."

Frederic Prokosch was ahead of his time in some ways. His career rose spectacularly and fell in early adulthood; the scope of his imagination—a particularly American imagination, it should be said—extended globally before globalization cast its spell upon contemporary literature; his historical and aesthetic sense invented a role for the melancholic ingénue before Millennials and Generation Z took the character mainstream. Most of all, Prokosch naturalized the absence of authority by the proliferation of standards in the public realm of letters. Neither his doctorate nor his pedigree meant much in the usual sense; he could achieve more fame and honors than his peers by simply making it all up, including, after a time, the credentials and bona fides. Nowadays dealers in facts have even worse noses for truths and untruths than previously. The many voices echo still, in our collective heads, from our mouths, on our screens.

12. A TALE OF THREE COLD WARRIORS

An important milestone, noted perhaps only by Cold-War afi-
cionados, is that three men central to the waging of that war all
died within the span of six months: George F. Kennan, Paul H.
Nitze, and Andrew J. Goodpaster.

Kennan is the best known of the three. During the Cold War,
Kennan received most of the credit for fathering the "containment"
policy that arguably won it. His death in March 2005 at 101 was
second only to that of Pope John Paul II in the number of obitu-
aries it inspired.

Nitze, who died in October 2004, aged 97, was less well
known than Kennan but hardly an obscure figure. His funeral at
the Washington National Cathedral was attended by more than
1,000 people. His career in and out of government extended from
the Truman to the Reagan administrations. Kennan's by contrast
ended in the mid-1950s, apart from a brief stint as John F.
Kennedy's ambassador to Yugoslavia. If Kennan gave us the outline
of a Cold War strategy, Nitze, in drafting much of what has become known as the most famous policy document of the era after
Kennan's "Long Telegram"—National Security Memorandum No.
68 (NSC 68) of 1950 on *United States Objectives and Programs for
National Security*—invented the mission for it. That was nothing
less than saving civilization from Soviet tyranny.

Kennan and Nitze were colleagues who did not always see eye
to eye. Kennan hated NSC 68, for example, claiming he never intended his plan of containment to be militarized to such an extent,

or to be extended beyond Europe. The document called for a three-to four-fold increase in defense expenditure. But they remained cordial, if occasionally wary of one another. Already the deaths of both men have been characterized as akin to those of John Adams and Thomas Jefferson in 1826: the yin and the yang of Cold War strategy—or as Nitze liked to put it, partners of a tension between opposites—uniting finally in death, the one following soon after the other.

This romantic picture is, unfortunately, a distortion. There is a third piece to the story, and a third figure, unknown but to a small but highly devoted group of insiders, who also died recently. Unlike Kennan and Nitze, Goodpaster, who passed away in May 2005, was a professional soldier, a four star Army General and former Supreme Allied Commander of NATO. He was also a close associate and friend of both men. It is impossible to understand the Cold War without including all three as intellectual poles of the same tent. There was not one policy, or two opposing doctrines, but rather a three-part synthesis which proved greater than the sum of its parts.

The person who deserves the most credit for grasping that synthesis was President Dwight D. Eisenhower. Goodpaster was his Staff Secretary—a position akin to today's National Security Advisor—and took part in nearly every meeting the President had, in addition to serving as his chief liaison to the foreign policy bureaucracy. It was not without justification that Goodpaster was known as "Ike's alter ego."

Stalin died soon after Eisenhower took office in 1953. There was much uncertainty over what and who would come next in the Soviet Union. The United States had just fought a costly war in Korea against Chinese and Soviet proxies; the Soviet Union now had its own atomic weapons; the Cold War had been militarized and globalized. NSC 68 was proving accurate indeed.

But Eisenhower would have none of it. Containment was a

compelling doctrine but Kennan's preferred tools—almost exclusively political and propagandistic—were no longer adequate. NSC 68 meanwhile provided minimal operational guidance. Full of dire predictions of world catastrophe, it did not offer a realistic blueprint for waging a long-term struggle against Communism apart from urging that the United States and its allies outspend and outman the Soviet Union at any given point of contestation around the world. It also offended Eisenhower's sense of fiscal prudence. He was obsessed with the potential for U.S. defeat through waste and largesse. He understood that the Cold War had to be fought on many fronts, not least of which was economic—hence the "military-industrial complex" against which he warned in his farewell address. Eisenhower was preoccupied with it throughout his two terms as president, not just at the end.

What was he to do? Eisenhower did something more than merely commission another policy blueprint. He decided to "game" it, that is, to set up three contending teams of advisers who would think through the implications of alternate policy approaches during the short, middle and long term. The effort began in the summer of 1953 and culminated several months later. Because it was conceived and took place partly in the solarium of the White House, it became known as the Solarium Project.

The Solarium Project and the principal policy document resulting from it—NSC 162/2—deserve to be remembered as one of the most significant group efforts in the history of U.S. foreign relations. If one judges historical significance by eloquence or bureaucratic noise, then Kennan's Long Telegram and NSC 68 should retain their prominent positions. But if one also includes the impact of a given policy on the ground, then the Solarium Project should rank equally high. Solarium's three teams played out the entire Cold War. In retrospect, they did not do too badly in anticipating, in 1953, the course it would ultimately follow. Taken together, they were remarkably prescient about the stakes for the

United States and sensible about the various tools it would need to prevail.

Each team comprised about ten members from various parts of the foreign policy bureaucracy along with a few academics from outside. Team A, headed conveniently by Kennan, was bound to a mainly political strategy toward the Soviet Union, focused primarily on Europe, and eschewed significant military commitments elsewhere. It also relied heavily on U.S. allies and placed a priority on alliance cohesion. Eisenhower gave Team B a similar mandate but allowed it to take a harder line towards the Soviet Union, and instructed it to contemplate policies that relied less on allies and more on the U.S. nuclear arsenal. It was given, therefore, a more unilateral mission, but one that nevertheless held to a clear line against taking direct military action within the Soviet sphere of influence. Team C was the "roll-back" team. Nitze was excluded from the project, but Team C's mandate was taken almost verbatim from the prescriptive passages of NSC 68: Diminish Soviet power—and Soviet-controlled territory—everywhere and by any means available. Eisenhower assigned Goodpaster to Team C, not because Goodpaster was known to sympathize with the roll-back approach, but because he trusted his aide's integrity and knew Goodpaster would ensure that Team C produced a solid report.

The results were exactly as Eisenhower had intended. Roll-back and NSC 68 were tossed into the dustbin of history, or at least until Ronald Reagan resuscitated aspects of them under very different circumstances. Solarium Project participants concluded that the logical result of a roll-back policy, in the context of the 1950s, would be catastrophic. Team A meanwhile proved to be effective at managing a united Western front but found itself too hamstrung by military weakness and shifting European politics, particularly in Germany. Team B came out somewhere in the middle: A growing nuclear arsenal kept the Soviets at bay but the United States found itself carrying the burden of Western defense alone.

Eisenhower then summarized the teams' findings in a presentation that Kennan said "demonstrated the President's intellectual ascendancy over every man in the room." Goodpaster asked: "Does that include you, George?" To which Kennan replied: "Yes it does, because only the President has proven himself able to grasp the full range of political and military aspects of the policies under consideration."

Debate over whether or how the United States won the Cold War will continue for decades; but it is certain that Eisenhower's synthesis made survival possible. He transformed an ambivalent doctrine of containment into a workable policy of deterrence. Kennan's preference for propaganda, covert action and political pressure was insufficient. Nitze's plan was too risky and inexact. The two approaches required a synthesis that deterred Soviet aggression while maintaining a common front with U.S. allies and limiting the domestic costs of a long and expensive struggle. The strategy, put forth in NSC 162/2, struck such a balance and proved enduring, not least because the diverse Solarium participants took part in a process designed for "each," as Eisenhower liked to say from his days at NATO, "in the presence of all."

The inner thoughts and conversations of the three men at this time are now lost. But the remainder of their lives suggests a pattern consistent with the role each played directly or indirectly in the Solarium Project. Each continued to both provoke debate, and contribute to consensus, over Cold War strategy. From his sinecure at Princeton, Kennan worked tirelessly to defend and redefine his understanding and prescription of containment in between writing several award-winning works of diplomatic history. Nitze continued to move in and out of government, serving as Secretary of the Navy and Deputy Secretary of Defense during the Vietnam era (when he became a closet dove), then resumed his earlier role as the leader of the Cold War hawks while negotiating nearly every major arms control treaty with the Soviet Union. Goodpaster went on to advise eight more Presidents, playing a quiet but critical role in the shadows, helping, for example, to convince Ronald Reagan to embrace Mikhail Gorbachev and his reforms, drafting the initial post-Cold War security arrangements for the states of Central and Eastern Europe, and helping the Pentagon plan for the overhaul of nuclear policy in the past couple of years.

The United States and the world survived the Cold War in part because these three men, and many like them, preserved the intellectual continuity that Eisenhower worried would be lost to political posturing. Each reminded leaders that there was no magic new strategy for meeting the Soviet challenge. U.S. interests required a careful blend: Kennan with the faith in diplomacy and political pressure; Nitze with military preparedness; and Goodpaster with the safeguarding of deterrence. Each man, in his own unique way, was simultaneously soldier, scholar and statesman. The world is a less safe place today without them.

SOURCES AND ACKNOWLEDGMENTS

Naming the sources for a book about influence brings to mind the historian A. J. P. Taylor's famous warning, "All sources are suspect," or, perhaps one more apt from the novelist James Branch Cabell: "Inasmuch as the characters and happenings of this book are all pilfered from fact, any incidental resemblance to fictitious events, or to imaginary persons, is unintentional." I am not a professional philosopher, psychologist, or anthropologist but a writer and occasional historian. So I'll spare the reader a long list of theoretical works on the nature, role, and perception of influence. What follows is a short list of sources that helped me in writing this book. All quotations that appear in the book come from them unless the speaker is otherwise identified.

Introduction

Achilles, Theodore. "Fingerprints on History." Occasional Paper. Edited by Lawrence Kaplan and Sidney Snyder. Kent: Lyman L. Lemnitzer Center for NATO Studies, Kent State University, 1992.

Achilles, Theodore. "How Little Wisdom." Unpublished manuscript. Courtesy of S. Victor Papacosma.

Pryce-Jones, David. *Signatures.* New York and London: Encounter Books, 2020.

Richardson, R. C., ed. *Images of Oliver Cromwell.* Manchester and New York: Manchester University Press, 1993.

Wright, Gordon. *Insiders and Outliers*. Stanford: Stanford Alumni Association, 1980.

Jean Monnet

Jean Monnet Papers. Fondation Jean Monnet pour l'Europe.

Duchêne, François. *Jean Monnet*. New York: Norton, 1994.

Hackett, Clifford. *Monnet and the Americans*. Washington, D.C.: Jean Monnet Council, 1995.

Kornblum, John. "Germany Changes But Not on Election Day." *Official Monetary and Financial Institutions Forum*, August 23, 2021.

Monnet, Jean. *Memoirs*. Translated by Richard Mayne. London: Collins, 1978.

Evangeline Bruce

Heymann, C. David. *The Georgetown Ladies' Social Club*. New York: Atria Books, 2003.

Lankford, Nelson. *The Last American Aristocrat*. Boston: Little Brown, 1996.

Sluga, Glenda, and Carolyn James, eds. *Women, Diplomacy and International Politics since 1500*. New York and London: Routledge, 2016. (This book includes another essay I've written about Vangie Bruce.)

Arminius Vámbéry

Landau, Jacob. "Arminius Vámbéry: Traveller, Scholar, Politician." *Middle Eastern Studies* 50, no. 6 (2014): 857–69.

Mandler, David. "Introduction to Arminius Vámbéry." *Shofar* 25, no. 3 (2007): 1–31.

Stone, Norman. "The Intelligence of Ármin Vámbéry." *Cornucopia* 10, no. 58 (2018): 26–31.

Vámbéry, Arminius. *The Story of My Struggles.* 2 vols. London: T. Fisher Unwin, 1904.

James Angleton

Latham, Aaron. *Orchids for Mother.* Boston: Little Brown, 1977.

Martin, David. *Wilderness of Mirrors.* New York: Harper, 1980.

O'Connell, Jack, with Vernon Loeb. *King's Counsel.* New York: Norton, 2011. (Vangie Bruce also makes an appearance in this book.)

Strausz-Hupé, Robert. *In My Time.* New Brunswick: Transaction, 1996.

Régis Debray

Bobkowski, Andrzej. *Wartime Notebooks.* Translated by Grażyna Drabik and Laura Engelstein. New Haven: Yale University Press, 2018.

Debray, Régis. *Empire 2.0.* Translated by Joseph Rowe. Berkeley: North Atlantic Books, 2004.

Debray, Régis. *Revolution in the Revolution?* Translated by Bobbye Ortiz. New York and London: Monthly Review Press, 1967.

Miriam Camps

Miriam Camps Papers. Mt. Holyoke College Archives and Special Collections.

Patel, Kiran Klaus. *Project Europe.* Translated by Meredith Dale. Cambridge: Cambridge University Press, 2020.

Van Middelaar, Luuk. *The Passage to Europe.* Translated by Liz Waters. New Haven: Yale University Press, 2013.

Russell Leffingwell

Russell Leffingwell Papers. Sterling Memorial Library, Yale University.

Benjamin Strong Jr. Papers. Woodrow Wilson Presidential Library & Museum.

Chernow, Ron. *The House of Morgan.* New York: Atlantic Monthly Press, 1990.

Erdmann, Andrew. "Mining for the Corporatist Synthesis: Gold in American Foreign Economic Policy, 1931–1936." *Diplomatic History* 17, no. 2 (1993): 171–200.

Lambert, Jeremiah, and Geoffrey Stewart. *The Annointed.* Guilford: Lyons Press, 2021.

Prins, Nomi. *All the Presidents' Bankers.* New York: Nation Books, 2014.

Swaine, Robert. *The Cravath Firm and Its Predecessors, 1819–1947.* Volume 1. New York: Ad Press, 1946.

Weisberger, William. "Leffingwell, Russell C." *American National Biography* (online).

Bryce Harlow

Burke, Bob, and Ralph Thompson, *Bryce Harlow.* Oklahoma City: Oklahoma Heritage Association, 2000.

Andrew Marshall

Augier, Mie. "Thinking About War and Peace: Andrew Marshall and the Early Development of the Intellectual Foundations for Net Assessment." *Comparative Strategy* 32, no. 1 (2013): 1–17.

Dayé, Christian. *Experts, Social Scientists, and Techniques of Prognosis in Cold War America.* Cham: Palgrave Macmillan, 2020.

Krepinevich, Andrew, and Barry Watts. *The Last Warrior: Andrew Marshall and the Shaping of Modern American Defense Strategy.* New York: Basic Books, 2015.

Kuklick, Bruce. *Blind Oracles.* Princeton: Princeton University Press, 2006.

Mahnken, Thomas, ed. *Competitive Strategies for the 21st Century: Theory, History, and Practice.* Stanford: Stanford University Press, 2012.

Mahnken, Thomas, ed. *Net Assessment and Military Strategy: Retrospective and Prospective Essays.* Amherst: Cambria Press, 2020.

Schutte, John. "Casting Net Assessment: Andrew W. Marshall and the Epistemic Community of the Cold War." Drew Paper No. 16. Maxwell AFB: Air University Press, 2015.

Meg Greenfield

Graham, Katharine. *Personal History.* New York: Knopf, 1997.

Greenfield, Meg. *Washington.* New York: PublicAffairs, 2001.

Also, the sources named above under Evangeline Bruce.

Frederic Prokosch

Greenfield, Robert. *Dreamer's Journey.* Newark: University of Delaware Press, 2010.

Prokosch, Frederic. *The Asiatics.* New York: Harper, 1935.

Prokosch, Frederic. *The Idols of the Cave.* Garden City: Doubleday, 1946.

Prokosch, Frederic. *Voices.* New York: Farrar, Straus, Giroux, 1983.

Vidal, Gore. *United States: Essays 1952–1992.* New York: Random House, 1993.

Tale of Three Cold Warriors

This essay was composed entirely from memory and not from any written sources, apart from the official documents mentioned in the essay. Nevertheless, the three warriors and several other figures in this volume make a more documented appearance in my earlier book, *The Atlanticists* (Santa Ana: Nortia Press, 2015).

Acknowledgments

I am grateful to the following people for being generous in years past with their recollections of this book's subjects: David Acheson, Daniel Arnold, Robert Bowie, Ben Bradlee, Kathleen Burk, Paula Bustos Castro, Henry Catto, Timothy Dickinson, Robert Ellsworth, James Goodby, Andrew Goodpaster, Lincoln Gordon, John Gray, Arthur Hartman, Wendy Hazard, Alex Hoyt, James Huntley, Rob King, Margot Lindsay, Éliane Lomax, Charles Maier, Christopher Makins, Ernest May, Richard Mayne, Kevin Mellyn, C. Richard Nelson, Henry Owen, Michael Pillsbury, Will Quinn, Rozanne Ridgway, Katja Seidel, Helen Soderberg, W. Scott Thompson, and Ellis Wisner. I am also indebted to Heather Yeung, who gave me the idea of writing it, and to Katie Godfrey and her crew, who produced it.

Earlier versions of chapters 7 and 11 were first published in Engelsberg Ideas (https://engelsbergideas.com/). Parts are reprinted here with the kind permission of the Axel and Margaret Ax:son Johnson Foundation. Chapter 12 was first published in the *NATO Review* (March 2006) and is reprinted here with the kind permission of the NATO Public Diplomacy Division.